THE RESTLESS QUEST

The Restless Quest

JULIAN N. HARTT

A PILGRIM PRESS BOOK FROM UNITED CHURCH PRESS, PHILADELPHIA

BR
85
.H29

Copyright © 1975 United Church Press
All Rights Reserved

No part of this publication may be reproduced, stored in a retrieval system, or transmitted
in any form or by any means, electronic, mechanical, photocopying, recording, or otherwise, without the prior permission of the publisher.

Library of Congress Cataloging in Publication Data

Hartt, Julian Norris.
  The restless quest.

  "A Pilgrim Press book."
  Includes bibliographical references.

  1. Theology—Addresses, essays, lectures. 1. Title.
BR85.H29   230   74-26836
ISBN 0-8298-0289-4

The scripture quotations are (unless otherwise indicated) from the *Revised Standard
Version of the Bible*, copyrighted 1946 and 1952 by the Division of Christian Education
of the National Council of Churches, and are used by permission. Biblical passages marked
NEB are from *The New English Bible, New Testament.* © The Delegates of the Oxford
University Press, 1961. Reprinted by permission.

United Church Press, 1505 Race Street,
Philadelphia, Pennsylvania 19102

CONTENTS

70115

INTRODUCTION

It appears that Christian theology of culture has run its course and is now either posted for interment or is on a siding waiting to be hooked on to some new philosophical train bound for Central City. How time flies and novel custom stales! Only yesterday, it seems, it was reported that God had died or had gone on sabbatical, but we were not to lose heart because there were really great and urgent things left on the theological agenda: the environmental crisis, an immoral war, the countercultural revolution, the raising if not the rearing of Consciousness, and, last but surely not least, Hope. Who of us theological sentinels and cultural assayers could then have dreamed that in short order the environmental crisis would be dissolved by an energy crisis, this nation's military involvement in southeast Asia would be terminated—more or less—by a once untamable falcon, and erstwhile revolutionaries would swoon in the light of transcendental meditation? Or that Hope would be a once-only thing?

So now it also appears that the velocity and frequency with which apocalyptic terrors streak up from below the horizon and plunge into the marrow of sensibility finds the theological sector with its categories down, whether they are Tillichian, Heideggerian, Barthian, Thomistic, or whatever. Thus discomposure pervades the theological camp; deservedly so, many feel. But are we so clearly entitled to surprise? Hardly. The good ship theology took on a radioactive cargo, its company attracted by the dazzle and dynamic of it all: Relevance, Historicism, several varieties of Analysis, Secularism—what a promising manifest! The point was that somewhere in the contemporary ethos there were uniquely modern canons of intelligibility with which to free the essential Christian message from the last elements of metaphysical, ethical, and mythological dross left over from less rigorous critiques. Thus theologians of culture hoped to make contemporary sensibility the touchstone, the dowsing rod, to discover a spirituality in which freedom and

9

creativity would unite to expel the last residue of authoritarianism from the life of faith. So even when theologians declared that the truths of the gospel were eternal, they hastened to declare, with equal if not greater conviction, that every expression of those truths is necessarily symbolic; and how shall it be said that there is a universal key to the symbols, even if one supposed that the symbols themselves were universal? The key must be sought in the spirit of the age.

Surely there is nothing intrinsically wrong, the faithless say, in a theological assay of the spirit of the age. The prime question about this has always been whether the theologians of the church are trying in that to determine what can be salvaged from the wreck of tradition: an essence, a residue, that the right-minded can accept—or at least treat with civility. Or are they, instead, seeking to let the light of the gospel illumine the actual condition of the mind and heart of the age? I believe that the latter is the proper course, however low its standings in the theological ratings. The Lord who speaks in and through the New Testament requires his followers to acknowledge where and what they are in the actual world. Confession of sin does not cover all that; nor does an affirmation of hope. Proper confession and affirmation of hope alike presuppose that one has been moved to them by authentic prophecy. So if one can prophesy only through the Spirit, it is also true that one can discern and appropriate authentic prophecy only through the Spirit. Authentic prophecy is never directed simply toward the rectification of the past; merely human efforts in that direction are indeed symbolic gestures only. Some such gestures are mandatory, but that is because the way forward can be rightly discerned and pursued only when bondage to time-bound idols has been canceled.

What then is authentic prophecy? That which allows a people to see the real fabric of their lives and days. That which empowers a people to mend what can be mended and enact a destiny rather than merely await it. It is from the authentic prophet we learn how Spirit-less we really are when we imagine that forgiveness is an ultimate rather than a transition, a qualifying test rather than a primary goal. Augustine speaks of the stage of his life when he prayed, O Lord, forgive my sins—but not quite yet. Did this mean that he was not yet ready to give up the sins for which nonetheless he craved to be forgiven? Perhaps. But perhaps he also meant that if he really accepted God's forgiveness he would find that the kingdom of God had become infinitely demanding as well as infinitely gracious.

So the prophet of the Lord always demands that something old come down to make place for something new. The Lord will build anew on burnt-over land, but he does not permit his kingdom to be treated as an annex to some contraption that pride or some other folly refuses to vacate. Jeremiah, for example, understood his prophetic vocation to include tearing down and building up, since there are things in the life of the people of God against which the Word of the Lord is an everlasting no! and there are things to which he says yes. If the authority of the prophet was challenged—as it was, often enough—the authentic prophet appealed to the Covenant which stands in the minds and hearts of the people of God as well as it grounds and overspans their history. Such prophets certainly do not stand forth as authentic simply because of charismatic gifts or because they are ethical pioneers in their own recognizance. Without exception they deny that the Lord has sent and commissioned them to start a new cult or fashion a new theology. They speak what God has commanded them to speak; they do what he has ordered. When they employ dramatic devices, their intent is not to dramatize themselves but the Word of the Lord and the desperate predicament of his people. It must therefore be the case that the faithful among the people of God are required to use their natural powers of discernment to grasp God's word in the prophetic performance, and thereafter their native intelligence in making proper applications of the Word to self and society. So to do are integral elements of God's demands through his prophets. Such demands are mortally hard to execute. That is why it seems so wonderfully comfortable to suppose that the Spirit does it all: inspired and energized the prophet; rendered his ordained hearers attentive; made them quick to obey, wise in that obedience; and eventually contrived a theological account of the whole business. But such comforts are specious. If Jeremiah had cause to complain vehemently about the exquisite hardships of his vocation, the people, his putative constituency, had some reason also to complain about their end of the prophetic affliction: to keep the faith when the Lord of the Covenant permits his people to be tossed to and fro on the tides of brutal imperial strife. Nobody in scripture admits that it is easy to be either the subject or object of authentic prophecy. Either way the natural resources of flesh and spirit have to be exercised to the breaking point.

I do not predict that the natural powers of human life will soon emerge into the theological world from under the Barthian eclipse. That widely advertised phenomenon was a superb feat of legerdemain. Confidence in it helped to identify and perhaps to make Barthians. It is not clear that Barth himself confused such attainments with the proper knowledge and service of God. Be that as it may, it is not written in the heavens that Barth was charged with the awesome assignment of legislating human natural resources out of revelation/faith, let alone out of human existence. To be sure, he hurled something like Jovian thunderbolts at that poor creature Natural Theology, but could he have fancied that he had put human reason once and for all in her place for every honest and faithful theological purpose? If so, he was afflicted with an errant fancy.

So I have ventured even to speak of the importance of a kind of reasoning inalienably involved in the knowledge of God. Angels do not need to use so pedestrian a power. We are not angels; nor are we beasts of the field. We are not destined to become angels, but now and forever it is wrong to suppress our unique human powers in the hope of becoming more successful animals. On such matters it is reasonable to dogmatize.

On the other hand, how can one overlook or try to look around the alarmingly deep salient in the line of truth driven (I mean the truth of faith) by philosophies as full of doubts about reasoning in great affairs as Barth's was? Traditional theism claimed too much for native rationality, even though the Christian metaphysicians of that stamp always admitted that the yield of that harvest was pretty thin, by no means sufficient to sustain the religious life. But now it seems that even that thin gruel is bootleg, and one set of marshals comes from Basel and another set from Oxford to empty the casks, and they vie with each other to prove which is the more invincible against any temptation to sample the goods before destroying them.

In the pieces taken together in this volume I have not ventured to make a direct defense of the metaphysics of traditional theism. I have in fact a modest budget of philosophic reservations about that viewpoint. These demurrers do not extend to or include the native powers of reason with which the Creator has seen fit to endow man—if I may be pardoned for weaving the eighteenth century into my own fustian. Put more positively, of all the times and scenes of my lifetime to date, the present ones are surely the last in which to recommend or tolerate passively the subordination of rationality to Intuition, Faith, Culture, Forms of Life, Linguistic Structures, etc., etc.: so many claims to messianic hegemony over the mind and heart of man. It is not enough to say that they cannot all be right. We must ask whether any of them is fit to rule.

An adequate determination of such issues requires the metaphysical plunge. That is, it is necessary somehow to penetrate to the very foundation of human being in the world if we are to have (ever or again) the right criteria for appraising multitudinous claims to truth, goodness, and power.

I find it hard to imagine or discover a historical situation in which this demand could have been more difficult to recognize, let alone meet. The present situation is a paralyzingly paradoxical one: We know more about the pluralities of cultures and cultural epochs than any age before ours, but we are not even sure that our scientific knowledge of these facts is *really* true. What we take to be its truth might only be a function of a time-bound perspective as arbitrary and contingent as that of the Epic of Gilgamesh. We are often invited, if not commanded, to acknowledge the impossibility of grasping what life "was really like then," so different are our frames of meaning from theirs. Of course there is a much lower-level question: Is it known whether the Epic "made sense" to the nonliterate multitudes of that lost world? Perhaps even then the Common Man said, "Can anybody understand what these theologians are saying? Do they expect us to accept that yarn as true?"

So on the one hand we have the loftiest advertisements of scientific knowledge as the highest achievement of the mind's cognitive thrust, and on the other an abysmal doubt as to whether "truth" is anything but a vacuous ideal floating over conceptual schemes whose fundamental principles we haven't the heart or mind to question so long as they inspire or warrant the technological transformation of the world out of the tyranny of scarcity into the imperialism of affluence.

In this paradoxical situation the Christian theologian has very few responsible choices. He can throw in his lot—and perhaps the fortunes of faith and church—with the dominant intellectual style of the age, or what, at any rate, he makes out to be that. There is no virtue in being so iron-headed as to deny a priori that any good for faith and church can come of that, Providence being what it is, and the imagination of theologians being what it is.

The alternative is to assert the necessity for the metaphysical plunge and argue for a range of its results. In the first instance the theologian assumes that the highest priority belongs to the analysis of religious language. In the second instance he asserts that somewhere in the theological agenda there must be a systematic effort to discover the relationships of human structures—linguistic and otherwise—to the structures and goings-on in the world.

I have said *assert* intentionally; it is not another way of saying *confess.* The theological confessionalist announces that he cannot but believe certain things to be true—*Hier stehe Ich, Ich kann nicht anders. . . .* But suppose one is standing on sinking sand? Should the rest of us be profoundly impressed by that one's asseveration that, after all, solidity is an illusion based on the fact that we sink at different velocities? Should we feel exalted by that one's proclamation that we sink now to rise later, and join him in confessing that the way down and the way up are only relativistic distinctions and in any case can be said to be God's doing?

Not that we need to feel timid about applauding the opposition of confessionalism to intellectual and spiritual arrogance. Credit where credit is due. But are we so sure that only confessionalism is compatible, as a theological stance, with religious, ethical, and political pluralism? Should we really suppose that the rights of persons and groups to be and do what they deem good and proper really depend on a general confession that sincere conviction, consistency, and resolute commitment are licensed surrogates for truth?

But what about such principles as integrity and consistency? In a cultural climate in which authenticity takes the place of truth, is the call to respect the integrity of the other person anything more than a demand that one should recognize the predicament of the other for what it is and thus neither judge it nor seek to change it? For all I know, the other has done the best of which he is capable. For all I know, he really sees the world as he confesses he does. For all I know, what he confesses is in fact the way the world really looks from where he stands —or sinks. But there it is: "For all I know" is in fact an appeal to ignorance.

So the confessionalist registers a tender regard for the integrity of others; also the assumption that others have distinctive angles of perception—how could they not if they are *really* others?—and distinctive interpretational filters. But what on confessionalist grounds can I allow the other as a warrant for claiming that what he sees is *really* there and the way he understands and expresses it is *really* right? It is one thing to confess one's partiality of perspective and sense all around an illimitable unknown. It is something else to legislate that condition for all mankind and name that vast unknown and unknowing the Real, the Absolute, or God.

Consistency does not deserve to come off much better than integrity. As an ideal it makes sense in a world that puts a great deal of capital into solidity, perdurability, rationality, substance, and the like. If, that is, ethical reality is perceived to be comprised of substantial moral characters, or at least of beings aspiring to that level of solidity, then the demand for consistency is intelligible: Behavior and professed principle ought to agree with each other; one ought not to alter or evacuate principle for the sake of comfort, success, peer acceptance, etc. But if people do not believe that ethical reality has that kind of solidity, if they believe "values are subjective" and causal explanation of preferences, choices, and decisions is omnicompetent, then to ask of self or other that one ought to honor principle—indeed, the same principle today that one professed yesterday—is wrong and wrong-headed. In fact in these latter days the behavior of public men strongly suggests a conviction in them that if the constituency does not remember what was professed and done in the past there is no reason now to admit that it *was* said or done. So they find it is both legitimate and necessary to question the motives of critics who insist that since the past is unalterably real there is a truth about it that is unalterably true; that is, cannot be modified or vacated either in the interest of national security or of personal power or privilege.

Now I take it that "the past is unalterably real" is an assertion and not a confession. So, also, "there is a truth about that past that is unalterably true." Assertions call attention to things that ought to be acknowledged and are not simply believed in or posited. And there are some assertions designed to call attention to fundamental realities: things, processes, and relationships we had better "consent to" unless we are prepared to let all certainty go. It is a recklessly venturesome soul who attempts that. Life on those terms is more wonderful than the hanging gardens of Babylon; it not only has no visible means of support, it has no real ones either.

Furthermore, it is a mistake to assume that since assertions are likely to be the game of unduly aggressive people in whom self-confidence reaches pathological levels, one is justified in treating assertions as disguised confessions. Be it noted that confessionalism can be asserted and argued for with as much bombast as *analogia entis,* Natural Law, or Verifiability. Perhaps it is true that theories and doctrines often suffer as cruelly from their protagonists as from their declared enemies. That is hardly sufficient warrant for backing away from the truth of what is true and confessing that one's history and the historical situation finally account for one's beliefs. Be it also noted, then, that assertions in principle are corrigible and confessions are not corrigible. True, I may confess something today that I did not confess yesterday, but yesterday's confession was all that I was capable of then (unless I am a liar, in which case all bets are scrubbed). So I have changed, but neither of the confessions is corrigible; each records what in fact I was and am constrained to believe. Nor as a confessionalist am I entitled to say that I have changed because the world has changed. Perhaps this is why confessionalists have a habit of asserting something like "God helping me I can do nothing else." Not that one has to believe in the traditional God in order to be a good confessionalist. But for that purpose one must posit something comparably absolute as justification of metaphysical doubt.

Of course it may be that in the end those who are saved are saved by faith. In the meantime—in which apostolic authority adjures us to work out our own salvation in fear and trembling—it is not blasphemous to doubt that there is anything in the least salvific in Luther's doctrine of faith, or Augustine's, or Barth's. For whatever of these one adopts, or for whatever one substitutes of one's own devising, a case has to be made. Psychological constraints, sociocultural endorsements, philosophical dominations—each of these, all of these, may appear in the case, but none of them is entitled to dominate it.

The realm of politics in the United States has particular importance for the Christian critique of culture. In the first place we have still to live with the old habit of seeing and using religion as a prop for the conventional value scheme. The slightly younger habit of seeing and using religion as an incentive, sanction, and warrant for overturning the conventional scheme is also still with us. These attitudes are dialectical twins—to a very considerable extent each rests on the assumption that the religious life is not in touch with a transcendent order of reality that imposes ethical-political mandates on the faithful or upon the whole order of society through the faithful prophets.

There is another important secular theological element in the national life. That is a revival of intellectual passion for Civil Religion. A cardinal dogma of this faith is the conviction that this nation has a unique destiny under God: We are a covenanted people, so a violation of covenant exposes the nation to grave peril.

This ethical-political reality is (was) as significantly celebrated in civil liturgy as in ecclesiastical. Some of us remember when Memorial Day—along with July 4 the high seasons in the civil-liturgical year—was as solemn and important a religious occasion as Christmas and Easter; if anything, the order of service on Memorial Day was more rigid than that of the great church occasions in the churches. The occasion was invariably celebrated in a building other than any of the churches: the theater, the hall of a fraternal order, or the high school auditorium.

Other elements of civil religion have fared rather better than those civil-liturgical ones: for instance, the conviction that true religion exists as an ideality diffused through secular society; so the *real* Christian is the good citizen whether or not he has any ecclesiastical loyalties—he could be a Parsee quite as fitly as he could be a Presbyterian. Thus the significant religious parameters are political-ethical rather than theological-creedal.

A new "Babylonian captivity of the church" does not strictly follow from these parameters, but there is an all but deadly probability of that implication. By and large today churches are listened to when public policy touches on sensitive moral issues, not because their leaders are known to be authentic prophets and seers of true righteousness but because ecclesiastical loyalties are still sometimes cashed out at the election booth.

We ought to find this situation profoundly disquieting only so far as it preserves an ancient and dishonorable religious-philosophical isolation of political power from ethical principles. That heresy thrives in American soil. It needs to be identified for what it is and opposed as stoutly as possible.

There is another element in America's civil theology that does oppose such heresies. That is the conviction that this nation is a uniquely covenanted enterprise. The weight and validity of this principle do not depend on a theory of the social contract or of a consentual foundation of the state, though, indeed, the principle may gain some reinforcement from such theories. The principle is that this nation is pledged, is bound by promise made before and unto God, to honor and defend justice, liberty, and dignity for all its people in perpetuity. It follows that wherever any of these—justice, liberty, and dignity—is denied to any of its people they in turn have a prima facie case against the State and not merely a general right vested in all mankind to arouse the conscience of others against suffering entailed by unmerited injury.

It is now popular in some quarters to point out that the founding fathers were by no means agreed that all the peoples of this continent and within the enforceable reach of the law of the State were full-fledged citizens and thus legitimate petitioners for its benefits. I own to perplexity as to why anyone should think that the ethical principles on which this nation is established were perfectly perceived and interpreted by the founding fathers or by any succession of leaders of the nation since. Suppose, for instance, that a social instrument I have devised is to cover or pertain only to human beings who are real persons; and I have a defective view of what makes for a real person; but I am sure that my view is sound and all right-thinking men in ages to come will embrace it. Is it conceivable that the ethical rightness and legality thereafter of that instrument should depend on my view of what makes for a real person? I think not. Moreover, even if I had intended that the benefits of that instrument should never be extended to the Iroquois because I believed them to be nonpersons—simply beastly simulacra of real human beings—all they would need in principle to do would be to show that an Iroquois can become, say, a good and true Christian, howling his wretchedness and need for God and true communion as pitifully as any Puritan whiteface to the manner born. Or he can learn to read the Constitution, the Holy Bible, the wit and wisdom of Cotton Mather; or meet any other description or designation of legal citizenship except to change the color of his skin. For that he would have to wait for the results of several generations of miscegenation provided on the one hand by the unbridled lusts of solid birthright Christians and, on the other hand, by the obviously just distinction between sexual congress with an Indian maiden and a heifer. On that count one may wonder why a dogmatically racist church never identified sex with an Indian or Black as bestiality.

We ought therefore to say that this nation as an ethical and legal commonwealth is not founded upon the psychological and philosophical limitations of its founding fathers but, rather, on the principles they espoused. No doubt many think these principles are also provincial and time-bound. Those presumptions are irrelevant to the consideration of the soundness and rightness of the principles. A moralist may be provincial: that is not a judgment upon his principles; it is a question about the kind of wisdom he may be able to bring to their application and interpretation.

Nonetheless it is very difficult to screen out every element of that pervasive spirit hailed and cursed as Relativism. For the element many sober people would judge to be the most provincial, oddly enough, in the minds of the founding fathers is their common conviction that Reason herself informed their principles as surely as Newton's laws informed the realm of nature. Not all of us suppose that we have said something ultimately dismissive in saying that they were typical products of the then young middle class in that they worshiped Property as much as Reason or God. Whether it was property rights or some other given of their time and place does not matter so much as their conviction that Justice was also a given, at once primordial and ultimate. Whatever our metaphysics, when we look at history we proclaim contingency; when we look at man we proclaim plasticity; when we look at nature we proclaim mechanical structure. These all arise to shout down every assertion of ethical universality.

But what instruction for soul and public policy is there in that cacophonous chorus? There's the question. Should we continue as a people to honor a political-ethical commitment (covenant) even if we believe that its historic rationale is a snare and a delusion? Should we say that what we are as a people is determined by something very like what ancient thinkers called Fate, but since there is no good reason for thinking that anything else is any better or for thinking that we can change our spots in any case, let us pretend that what we are is what we have chosen to be: let us pretend that "Liberty for all!" is something we believe in because we see that it is right and it would be right despite our denials of it?

I believe that some things can be seen and defended as right, and that that belief itself is capable of rational defense. I do not suppose that I have provided a defense that will stun its opponents or fill posterity with speechless wonder, but the defense of such a view is a noble cause for which to go under.

A few years ago we were hearing a good deal about the importance of creating and fostering an indigenous American theology, something in which it was evident that the hegemony of Germanic modalities had at last yielded not to some abridgment of Oxbridge philosophy but, rather, to something in the theological line that faithfully reflected the unique qualities of Christian experience in our own history. I thought then and do still that this aspiration was sound if its realization did not tip the faith and life of the churches sympathetic to it toward theological chauvinism. We used to hear then, too, that Karl Barth considered American theology a very poor show, hardly worth the trouble to ignore. I have no idea whether he really felt that: I should think the matter was important for biographical purposes, perhaps, but surely irrelevant for theological purposes except, just possibly, for the purposes of political theology; that is, for religious concepts and theories of the state. This is an area in which I find Barth notably uninstructive. It is an area in which "the American experience" may have something to contribute.

But not unless theologians can steer around the twin monsters of

chauvinism and historicism. Whether or not I have successfully nego-
tiated those waters, I have no doubt at all it can be done. For in order
to understand what the political covenant of this nation is, one does
not need to participate in it; nor does one need to do that in order to
weigh the arguments advanced for abrogating that covenant, or for
modifying it properly to cover all the people of this land, or for standing
pat on it just as it is (on the assumption that we know just what it is).
So also for the explicit religious dimension: The covenant is executed
before God. Here the appeal is not to One who can and will make us
keep the promise—a promise is exactly the sort of thing one cannot be
made to keep—but to One to whom the intent of all promises is open;
he is the supreme promiser. Thus "before God" ought to call attention
to the depth and inclusiveness of the intention: There is no ulterior
motive behind it; it is binding until time ends in God or the nation
expires from the effects of some less cosmic occurrence.

As a nation every people lives under a "restricted covenant"; the State
does not exist to serve all mankind nondifferentially. For some thinkers
that is enough to liquidate the morality of the State. I do not accept
that view, but who can seriously deny that in our time the military and
economic power of the United States has had worldwide scope? Must
we not say, then, that while this nation has no moral responsibility for
looking after the well-being of mankind as such, it has to use its power
under prudential restraints so profound and delicate that only a thinker
enthralled by the rhetoric of power politics would refuse to call them
moral? That rhetoric is an impressive social fact; the realities it is supposed to comprehend have passed beyond its ken.

Thus once again the notion of the restricted political-ethical covenant
requires to be set under the canopy of universal moral interests. For what
one may pardonably (that is, defendably) take as the great tradition in
political theology always held that the state had to answer not only for
the way it behaved in relation to its subjects, how it treated their human
rights and powers, but also for the way it behaved in relation to other
states. Now for the great powers—indeed, notably for the greatest
—policies of the state must have a due regard not only for the present
community of mankind but also for generations as yet unborn. So the
right of the state to defend itself against aggressors does not include the
right to render the planet incapable of supporting human life. The state
never had that right, of course, but there was no point in mentioning
the matter until some state had that power or something terribly close
to it. Now that power exists, and as a people we are obliged to wonder

whether moral suasion alone can successfully inhibit its exercise. The future of humanity depends on what "moral suasion" properly and effectively includes. This is a theme worth the prayers of all Christians everywhere and the devoted attention of people interested in political theology.

I take this occasion to register my esteem, affection, and gratitude for two former colleagues, Robert Lowry Calhoun and H. Richard Niebuhr. They were my teachers, but they are not to be debited with any of my views.

Charlottesville, Virginia

THE RESTLESS QUEST

I

1

Prophecies, Priorities, and Packages

I

The scene is full of prophets; the air is dense with prophecies. And in what diversity! Astrologers continue to do a big business, but other kinds of prophecy are more likely by far to land on the front page and to make it with Walter Cronkite. I am thinking of two kinds of prophecy in particular. After giving a brief characterization of each of these two modes of prophecy, I shall then ask you to concentrate with me on one of them.

A. The first of these commanding modes of prophecy makes much of the reign of law in nature and in human history. So far as prophets of this persuasion indulge in prediction, they appeal for that purpose to the necessary consequences of the breaking of law. Here in abstract formula is this mode of prophecy:

1. If X is the case, Y will follow.
2. X is the case; therefore Y will follow.

Now put this as a concrete affair:

1. If we continue to pollute the air and the earth and the water, more and more people will die from one or another poison and our children's children will inherit a stinking desert.
2. We are in fact continuing to pollute air, earth, and water. So more and more of us can count on dying from one or another poison absorbed from the environment. And the city becomes each passing day more of a stinking desert.

B. The second mode of prophecy can be expressed in this abstract formula:

1. If X is the case, I will do Y.
2. X is the case, so I will do Y.

Now here it is in concrete historical form:

Hear this, you heads of the house of Jacob and rulers of the house of Israel, who abhor justice and pervert all equity, who build Zion with blood and

Jerusalem with wrong. Its heads give judgment for a bribe, its priests teach for hire, its prophets divine for money; yet they lean upon the Lord and say, "Is not the Lord in the midst of us? No evil shall come upon us." Therefore, because of you Zion shall be plowed as a field; Jerusalem shall become a heap of ruins.—Micah 3:9-12

Where the first mode of prophecy calls attention to an unbreakable law, the second points to the operation of an invincible will whose righteous demands have been adequately communicated to the party of the second part. Both modes are committed to uncovering the actual condition of a presumptively favored people, for both operate from the assumption that the truth has been long concealed by pious lies. But for the first mode it does not greatly matter that these lies and deceits are an offense to heaven, while for the second mode this is what matters most. It matters most because God has bound himself in a promise to human life, and this promise is a two-way street; the supreme richness of life is available to man only if he also binds himself in promise or covenant to the same God who loves all. Thus the future is not under the rule of law; it too is bound in the power of a promise. What God promises shall come to pass, simply because God is God.

II

I propose now to concentrate on the second mode of prophecy for two reasons: It is closer to the dominant religious traditions of our world, and it is a more powerful attack on the American conscience, religious and otherwise. More powerful. Whether it is more just is another matter.

The (B) prophet does not really begin with "If." He says, "The System is wrong, man; the Big Package, baby, is rotten to the core." He does not mean that all of it is bad. Even the most radical prophet is grateful for the audience provided by the mass media—and the mass media are part of that Big Package. And he needs freedom of speech and freedom of movement to get on with his job—and people willing to endow him. But he *does* mean that the *package* is wrong, so even the good things in it are infected. The supermarket wraps things in clear plastic so you can see what you are buying, and that is good, right? Wrong. You can't see the fat on the bottom. And you can't smell the meat until it is too late.

What then is really wrong with the Big Package, the System? It has fouled up the priorities. First things do not appear in it in their right place, if at all. So of course other things are out of place and out of order.

Worse still, the System is advertised as not only the most powerful and the richest in the world but as the best, too. But when we say, "Good! That means we can afford to do anything that will improve life for everybody on the short end!" we are promptly told, "Not so. First things first. First ABM, the moon, new highways—preferably laid out to put another chunk of the ghetto under asphalt—new buildings, etc., etc. Then whatever is left over can be used for the people left out." In the meantime many more will be forced off the short end of the stick, and more and more will be converted to the proposition that the whole stick had better go.

So the prophets try to convince us that the Big Package has terribly jumbled the priorities. It is slick, this package, but it is rotten. It is squeezing human life into impossible shapes. It is draining simple humanity out of more and more people. Good with products, the system is poor with persons; rich in things, poor in soul. Therefore the system must be changed. Human interests and capacities and rights and duties must be repackaged. There must be a reordering of priorities.

No doubt we have many questions for these prophets, such as: How do *you* know so much about priorities? What raises you so far above the moral level at which the rest of us live? What makes you think you are any less self-righteous than the rest of us? If you are so interested in purifying the system, why don't you start by taking a bath? If you really are committed to changing the atmosphere around here, why don't you begin by changing your shirt?

These questions make for a lively conversation. Nevertheless, we might profitably consider a somewhat different question, and not for prophets alone but also for those who zealously stone them. This is the question: Why do we commonly assume that if priorities could be straightened out, the formation of a new and better package would more or less take care of itself? I want to suggest a simple and perhaps simpleminded answer to that question. Then I shall invite you to consider another question for the prophet and for ourselves.

III
We have in the New Testament a capital reason for the grand prophetic assumption that from sound priorities come sound packages. Here is a recent translation of it: "Set your mind on God's kingdom and his justice before everything else, and all the rest will come to you as well [Matt. 6:33, NEB]."

In its own context the phrase "all the rest" refers to food, shelter, clothes—the physical essentials. It hardly refers to social status, power, fame, pomp, adulation—the things which preoccupy favored Americans. But be that as it may, we can see how this prophetic teaching encourages us to believe that if our hearts are trained upon the highest good, lesser things will fall into proper place; they will come either as the natural consequence of being good or because God in his heaven will hand them out as appropriate rewards. In either case it is fatally easy to fix attention upon the goodies and convert goodness, or the good reputation, into the price we must pay in order to enjoy the goodies. Thus the prophetic critics of this social system may be very close to truth when they declare that the system takes even the most sublime counsel concerning the priorities and subverts it, making it over into something like "Take care of the church and God will take care of you!" One wonders how many generations of Christians have supposed that they could tithe their way into God's everlasting favor. Perhaps they have misunderstood or just simply misheard scripture; for scripture has it that God loves a cheerful giver, not a calculating one.

But now I should like to suggest that the Package and the prophet in their acrid confrontations encourage us unwittingly to overlook a very important element in this same word from the New Testament. It is this: There is a way of passionately seeking and resolutely serving the good of others that brings into sight the human commonwealth as such as a high-priority object of love and loyalty. Say, rather, the highest priority, because God, as well as wise and just men, loves that commonwealth without reservation. Therefore, he is true prophet who strives to bind upon love and conscience that human commonwealth as a promise to be kept whatever the cost. Christians believe that so far as Jesus reckoned the cost of his life and consented to it, he is uniquely Son of God, as well as prophet.

IV

Now another question arises for the prophet: How ought we to redo the priorities? What ought to come first?

At this point our contemporary prophets may turn into messiahs, each saying, "I am the answer; I have things rightly sorted. So follow me and you shall really live, man!"

But there are so many of them, and they offer such widely divergent visions of the blessed life. Undoubtedly we ought to consider ourselves truly fortunate to have on the scene at the same time Norman Mailer and Billy Graham, and Hugh Heffner and Herbert Marcuse. But they can't all be right—on that they are all agreed, and so are we.

Then what are we to do? Since I am neither a prophet nor a messiah, I can only fall back on a prudential prescription: "Test every spirit!" Test every prophecy and everyone who cries, "Here at last is the kingdom of everlasting beauty, peace, and joy!" Test each and all by asking: Does it enhance my capability for relating myself to the human commonwealth freely, creatively, and hopefully? Does a prophecy bring again into clarity promises made and promises broken? Does a way beyond betrayal and fraudulence begin to appear?

When such questions can be answered knowledgeably and clearly with an honest affirmative, we are in the presence of true prophets, whether or not they are good clean All-American boys. They may not have all the wisdom we need to straighten out the priorities and produce an honest and humane package. But their work is God's work if they kindle imagination, and help us to stretch ethical muscle we have never used before, and engender patience (as much patience with others as we have generally for ourselves), and make us see again the thousand unexpected places where clear vision and quiet courage can win small but real victories for humanity.

V

Yet some will say, "This takes us only as far as the kingdom of Man. Surely a Christian preacher ought to put in a good word for the kingdom of God, which to love and serve is the highest priority of all."

Well, I think I have. For the kingdom of man is an object of God's love. And his justice is extended over it; we cannot run out from under that canopy. His love embraces the human commonwealth. For its healing God offers his own life. He has so promised. Above all others he is faithful in promise.

But heed, then, the faithful prophet. God does not passively endure the violation of Man. He does not smile or yawn or doze or look the other way when the human realm is raided, looted, dishonored, defaced, and sold into captivity. Walls created by human hands to keep people in—or, for that matter, to keep them out—are an offense to the righteous God, for these are walls of alienation; and they shall all come down. That is high up on God's priorities. That too is a promise he will keep.

VI

Ever so many of us are now weary of prophets and prophecies. Do we feel quite so fed up with the conditions against which God in every age raises up prophets and appoints them to tear down in order that something better might be built? Perhaps we are not as weary of prophets as we are of the bad conscience they leap upon with hobnailed boots. For this nation, this Big Package, was built upon a great promise: that in it all should be treated as equals, whoever they were, wherever they came from. That promise has often been broken. With regards to some people it was never kept, and it has not yet been kept.

Is, then, such a promise still in force? I believe it is. It was made before God. I believe God heard it and approved it. And that means there is an immense backing for the promise made by our forefathers.

So whether or not we are weary of prophets and prophecy, we had better be moving out; for we have many miles to travel and many promises to keep.

2

The Philosopher, the Prophet, and the Church

Whoever aspires to treat so large a subject at once encounters formidable problems. For instance, should he take a sympathetic stance within each role, so far as he is able, viewing each from within as well as from the perspectives of the others? Or should he take a neutral position from which to sketch defining structures and relations? Provisionally, I venture to do the latter. A risky venture, no doubt, for one of the other of these roles may be unwittingly assumed thereby; or one may find that he has projected for himself a role rather like that of a tightrope artist who would sally forth across a chasm without benefit of balance pole—or rope.

A further problem appears. Does not such a project claim implicitly for itself the right to assign cultural tasks and responsibilities to philosopher, prophet, and theologian? Etiquette may set limits to such claims; but one may suspect, beneath civility, ambition that vaults too high. Yet this risk is to be embraced, not without caution, in the hope that, from the descriptive analysis that follows, normative inferences will not parade illicitly in the garb of necessity.

If, then, näiveté or brashness carry us around (if not through) these initial problems, at what point is an actual beginning of our program to be made? A beginning is made by suggesting several interpretations of the philosopher's role in culture.

1. The philosopher may be viewed as the point or moment at which a culture rises to purest consciousness of itself. Has anybody except Hegel ever so conceived and expressed the role of the philosopher in culture? Well, perhaps to him the ambiguous honor falls of having expressed this view in its starkest and most ambitious terms; but Hegel did not invent this state of mind, he did not conjure it from nowhere,

This chapter is reprinted from *Journal of Religion*, XXXV, No. 3 (July 1955). © Copyright 1955 The University of Chicago. Used by permission.

and in other guises and forms it survives Hegel and the quarreling descendants who have plucked his bones clean and white.

Imagination need not be strained to invent paradoxes with which to harass this view; they are built into it; the system comes already equipped with them. For instance, the moment of purest self-consciousness which culture has of itself would seem to be wholly devoid of the thrust and passion of cultural creativity. The philosopher *understands* the creative spirit; the creative spirit through the philosopher reflects upon itself; but the business of creation is over. Has not the Master himself said it: "The owl of Minerva takes its flight only at the close of day"? But what an odd result for a philosophical systematic so chastely rational! The culture creators are inadequately rational—the idea is in them, but it is deficient in respect to self-consciousness. The philosophers are adequately rational, but they are deficient in respect to creative powers. Nietzsche has his own answer to this: The "rational" man is one who in respect to creativity is—a eunuch!

The Hegelian mood is softened with time's passage, but it is not erased. Collingwood reflects it, in our own day. Collingwood believes that the philosopher is concerned with the absolute presuppositions of a culture. These absolute presuppositions are the principles and beliefs upon which that culture rests. Whether or not the philosopher plays a significant (to say nothing of a decisive) role in the actual formulation of these absolute presuppositions, Collingwood does not seem to have a clear word to say. Does he suppose that these basal principles and beliefs arise magisterially out of a cultural unconscious (that is, from a source in a way unresponsive to rational expectations and mandates and directives)? I am constrained to interpret Collingwood thus. It would not follow that the philosopher was thereby reduced to an insignificant role in culture. The philosopher plays an indispensable role in helping his culture to understand itself. But to understand is not necessarily to enjoy an efficacious transcendence in relation to what is so understood. Indeed, Collingwood expressly denies to the philosopher, and presumably to anybody else, this kind of transcendence in relation to his culture.

We must not imagine that this first general point of view concerning the philosopher's role in culture is a closed Hegelian preserve. Others hunt there also who would not dream of stating their convictions in the grandiose terms of the Hegelian system and mood. Something of the essential spirit of the viewpoint survives even where the fundamentally positive and affirmative mood of Hegel has given way to a mood vastly different. The affirmative mood surrenders to a problematic mood.

The "problematic mood" of (1) is the phase in which the philosopher is, above all, aware of the critical and decisive problems in and for a culture's self-understanding.* In the contemporary scene this mood is expressed by philosophers as different from each other as the methodologists and the existentialists. Each of these groups exhibits great internal diversity. Positivists, instrumentalists, semanticists—it were thankless, even if it were possible, to call a roll to which all the methodologists could or would respond. But one thing is true of them all, so far as they evince any serious desire to be numbered with the philosophers: *The problems with which they are concerned are regarded, at least by them, as important for the health of our culture.* (Perhaps this is an overly optimistic generalization, but is it not permitted to sin on the side of charity?) To be sure, there are some who would disclaim such unsolicited and unearned honor; and they sometimes most assiduously cultivate the impression that they "do" philosophy for no better reason than other men play cricket or train seals. One wonders whether good cricket players and seal trainers really share this sporting attitude toward their respective interests.

Again, so far as we can say that there is an existentialist conception of the role of the philosopher in culture, we can also say that "problematic" suggests the mood. What is problematic in the first order is *being*. But culture also is a vast reflection of the precariousness and transitoriness of existence. The "plain man" may be unaware of (or at least inattentive to) his real situation, but the philosopher knows what this situation is, and it is his calling to interpret it. This he can do because the "situation" is not merely the circumstance and condition of the "private person."

In the existentialist expression of the problematic mood, there is a powerful threat to the whole notion of the philosopher as the moment of culture's purest self-consciousness. This threat is the quest for a positive ontological foundation for the whole philosophical enterprise; being itself transcends and embraces all the idiosyncrasies of individual disposition and behavior and every product and aspect of culture.

Naturally, this threat is felt and transmitted in many degrees of intensity and clarity. Yet even its muted and obscure expression is not to be interpreted naïvely as a product of the culture-relativizing impulses

---

* "Above all" means both that the philosopher is more aware of these problems than he is of anything else and that the philosopher is more aware of these problems than anybody else is; or, at the least, he expresses his awareness more clearly than anybody else does— more clearly, but not necessarily more vividly or more powerfully.

running so strongly through contemporary life. Some of the nihilistic quality of existentialism can be fairly interpreted as resistance to just these culture-relativizing tendencies. This is true of Nietzsche, and it is true of Sartre.

Nietzsche celebrates the passing of the gods. Who or what are these gods? They are the arch-values of Western culture deified, that complex of Christian, scientific, democratic, equalizing attitudes and forces which, in Nietzsche's eyes, had throttled and corrupted the creative powers of Western man.* These gods must go. Indeed, Zarathustra says, they have already departed; they are even now dead. We need not linger to inquire whether the "now" of their demise is the futuristic present of the seer or whether for Nietzsche the root problem is not really the gods—they come and go—but the human proclivities for deification. What is of greater interest in this context is Nietzsche's discovery that Western culture binds the creative spirit to the golden wheel of necessity; all its significant manifestations are immanently determined by the absolute. Christian theologians talk of God Transcendent; but as they tell it this God of Gods and Lord of Lords determines all human emprise by immanent operation, not simply by far-off, eternally condign purpose. Thus the Christian doctors customarily invoke necessity with a softer name; and Hegel blandly calls it "freedom."

Sartre has his own antirelativizing program, even though he is supposed by many to be the most perversely and profoundly nihilistic of the existentialists. Some of his critics have been misled by a confusion of society and culture, and this is their confusion at least as much as it is his. True, Sartre will grant to neither society nor culture a foreordaining essence which transcends and binds the will of the person. To do so would, in principle, abrogate freedom, whether or not piety or good sense helpfully confused the issue at the practical level. But it would be absurd to conclude from this that there are, for Sartre, no structures of human relationships and no cultural creations of which some account must be given both theoretically and concretely and to which some response must be made. On the other hand, to look upon one's self as but the bearer of culture and upon all one's decisions as simply effects of social conditioning would be, as Sartre sees, to enter a specious plea for release from responsibility. There is about me a world I never made by conscious operation of my will; but this world, objectively impervious to my will's assault and impregnable against all the thrusts of my feeling, has not made me, either.

---

* Cf. Heidegger, "Nietzsches Wort 'Gott ist tot,' " in *Holzwege*.

We began with a Hegelian view of the philosopher's role in culture. The existentialist quest for an ontological ground for the entire philosophical enterprise appears as a powerful threat to this viewpoint. Let us now suppose, for the sake of the argument, that this threat proves widely and deeply destructive to this first view. What alternative view is forthcoming?

2. Ontology is the ultimate foundation for the interpretation of culture and therefore of the philosopher's role in culture. The function of the philosopher is to interpret the ontological ground of culture. But what does this mean? Since it is the existentialist who has carried us hither, I suggest that we see what he can tell us at this point. First, then, "ontological" means two rather different things: (a) a doctrine concerning being, and (b) the nature and structures of being itself, the latter being sometimes designated the "ontic," that about which the "ontological" is propounded. Thus (a) has certainly to do with (b), but, according to the existentialist, the philosopher has some more serious role than to propound doctrines of being and to demonstrate how the primary aspects and creations of culture all reveal ontological judgments. Yet the actual ontic ground of culture is nothing that can be taught as a body of doctrine can be taught. The ontic ground can only be concretely and incommunicably intuited. If this is so, the philosopher, in addition to having his own intuitions, can make his philosophy exemplify or otherwise express these ontic intuitions; and he can tell how a culture looks to him on the basis of these intuitions.

Even on existentialist grounds, the role of the philosopher is not necessarily exhausted by what has just been stated. What is disclosed to the ontic intuitions may be structures and powers which are "really there." What is incommunicable is the personal quality of the process whereby these structures and powers are apprehended. Communication does not establish or transmit these ontic structures and powers; at the most, communication can help to focus and to clarify attention to them.

So much for existentialist asseveration. There are others who subscribe to (2) with an equal passion, e.g., the Thomists. We need hardly remind ourselves that, as this second general viewpoint is elaborated by the Thomists, it becomes a lash for the backs of the cultural relativists. Indeed, I suppose that, on Thomist terms, to correct or to counteract such gross and influential error is part of the role of the philosopher. Or, to put the matter in more positive terms, the philosopher is concerned with the "jointings" of truth, goodness, and beauty with being, at the upper limits of generality. From here the Thomist philosopher may sally forth on critical foray into some particular realm, e.g., poetry, or into the arts as a whole. But qua philosopher he hardly has intimate concern for the details of principle and practice in these realms. Nor does he rightly serve, qua philosopher, as a *reformer* of culture and society. Reformer and philosopher may dwell within one human frame; but their conversation with each other is often noisy, sometimes violent, rarely edifying.*

Are we then egregiously mistaken in supposing that some philosophers as philosophers have something very like the stance of reformers? This is no mistake, egregious or otherwise. The philosopher does sometimes take up arms against error, falsehood, and iniquity. He becomes upon occasion a militant, seagoing critic of the culture about him. As some see the philosopher's role, he has here violated the terms of this license. These critics of the philosopher as reformer would say that the philosopher should have it in mind to understand that culture and to describe its nature: his not to deride, or to condemn, or to praise. With what right, then, does he pass from a phenomenological-descriptive attitude toward culture into a prescriptive attitude? (This is a philosophical question, not just a psychological and a biographical one.) And with what right does the philosopher move from prescriptive principles out into the routes of policy formation and policy decision?

These are questions important enough to be asked without prejudice. They are questions which open up the whole problem of what a philosophical critique of culture really is. I believe we can safely and quickly grant that the philosophical critique of culture is significantly different from other forms of cultural criticism. Philosophical critique goes to the ontic and ontological foundations of the human situation as such. Or perhaps we should say the *ultimate* philosophical critique, in order to distinguish it from aesthetics, philosophy of science, philosophy of religion, etc. This is the distinction: in aesthetics, for example, the philosopher is primarily involved with the delineation of the structures which are called "significant forms" and with the creative processes in which these forms emerge and are related to one another. But an ultimate philosophical critique undertakes to show how the art of a people expresses the truth-and-error of its total, its organic, appropriation of the ontic ground of the human situation. Truth-and-error, yes, because

---

* What is to be made of Descartes in this connection? Certainly, here is a philosopher profoundly concerned for the foundations of Western culture and one persuaded that something is significantly wanting from those foundations which he can supply, which to do is his calling as philosopher. But he does not say that society must be reconstituted and transformed. And he does not set his hand to the practical tasks involved in such a reconstitution or arouse and inflame others to do so.

where the philosopher aspires to an ultimate critique of a culture, he seems always to discover that there is truth and error in that culture's appropriation of the ontic ground. The conclusion is therefore irresistible: every culture seriously misapprehends and misinterprets its relation to "ground." Is this to say that every culture distorts and arbitrarily delimits human nature and its possibilities? No, the two assertions cannot be substituted for each other. If the latter is asserted, it must be asserted on some other evidence.

We cannot elude a further inference. The misapprehension and misinterpretation in every culture's view of its relation to ontic ground lie not alone in human nature considered in abstraction but in the essential relation of this human nature, considered concretely, to the ontic ground. An ultimate philosophical critique of culture makes this essential relation a primary object of scrutiny and reflection. And so far as such a critique incorporates both prescriptive principles and appropriate routes for determination of policies, these principles and routes must lie within, or follow cogently from, the philosopher's ontic intuitions and not from that culture's own beliefs and pretensions concerning the ground. The philosopher uses the "languages" (the relevant symbolic systems) of his cultural epoch to express his ontic intuitions. But the ultimate presuppositions and principles of his critique of culture go deeper than these language structures. Where he ventures some kind of discursive proof for his claims, the real business of such proof is done before the proof is more than launched. *The proof is really the structure by which the philosopher passes from ontic intuition out toward prescriptive principles and the determination of routes for policies.* Without such structures ("proof bridges"), an ultimate philosophical critique of culture is rightly condemned as arbitrary or as visionary or as simply unintelligible and irrelevant.

In principle, then, our questions concerning the passage from the descriptive to the prescriptive (in a philosophy of culture) are answered. This passage is accomplished by discursive reasonings whereby the meaning of ontic intuitions is explicated. But in addition to this we must note that the phenomenological-descriptive attitude is but part of the scaffolding of a philosophical critique of culture. The inner life of such a critique is revealed only in answer to the question: What *is* it that is phenomenologically grasped? The answer is: *patterns and structures produced and assumed by creative spirit wrestling with its ultimate ground.* Out of this wrestle, good and evil, right and wrong, are born, in myriad form and quality amid the welter of cultures. The philosophical critique of culture is calculated to show how the good-and-evil of a particular culture expresses the ethos of that culture, and, beyond this, how the ethos itself is an encounter with the ground. But the critique goes far beyond a mere indication of how culture has in fact grasped being and world; it precipitates the question as to how this culture might be healthier, saner, more productive. This question is precipitated out of the philosopher's own encounter with being and world. Out of such encounter the philosophical vocation is derived, so far as the philosopher is seriously involved in and concerned for the human enterprise around him.

The philosopher is not the only one who proposes an ultimate critique of culture. On this stage a strange and striking figure appears: the prophet. I say "appears" as though the prophet were our contemporary. To speak so may seem inflated rhetoric, since we usually suppose that the prophet is confined to the Old Testament, except perhaps for some figures in the early church who are hardly prophets in the same sense. I should like to be indulged in this whimsy of rhetoric for the present. Perhaps authentic prophecy is not to be confined to the Old Testament, even though we do not expect to see God-haunted Amos preaching from the street corner ordinarily held down by the Salvation Army band.

In the Bible the prophet does not speak in terms of ontic intuitions. He does not appear to be concerned with culture as such. He speaks of the will of God expressed in and visited upon a people as judgment and as redemptive solicitude. These differences in mode of expression undoubtedly reflect wide differences in fundamental orientation between philosopher and prophet, but we ought not to magnify and crystallize the division of labor, so that we make of the philosopher a (Promethean) hero of reason and of the prophet a hero of obedience and faith. When the prophet hears the "word of the Lord," he is dealing with ontic intuitions; the Lord whose voice he hears is the creator of all men and the judge of all the earth, in whose hand all the nations are held. When the prophet declares that God alone is God and that God has but one standard of righteousness, justice, and mercy for all men, he is dealing with what is "really out there"; he is not the advance propaganda agent for a cultic hegemony.

Yet the prophet is not really a philosopher in goatskin. The prophet is much more intimately and essentially involved with the reconstitution and transformation of a people's life. He is not moved to delineate the structures and processes arising out of man's relationship to the ontic ground. *Above all, he deals with the categorical policies which are de-*

manded by the living utterance of the living God. "Categorical policies" is a phrase which designates those specific things which the people must do now in order to bring society and private aspiration into the "charter" of the community. Two things about these categorical policies are particularly interesting and important: (a) they are thrown out by the prophet without reference to broad prescriptive principles, such as the Decalogue, and (b) the prophet obviously relies upon the traditions (or at least what he believes to be the defining traditions) of his culture in a way significantly different from anything exhibited by the philosopher relative to his culture. These two things merit some special attention.

a. The prophet does not derive categorical policies from broad prescriptive principles. This does not mean that these principles are lacking from his contemporary culture; it means only that they are not the essential point of departure for his vocation. Certainly the people know what God demands; if they are now stupid, theirs is the stupidity of sottishness, and sottishness is no excuse before God. But this knowledge of God's demands is not laid down in general moral theory or in universally prescriptable laws or rules. God's word is everywhere and always a *living* word. His will has been made known through devoted flesh and blood. Seers, poets, kings, and judges, these are some of the letters in the alphabet of divine communication. And now God speaks again in and through the prophet, who, on his own recognizance, is a "new" letter ("I am neither a prophet nor a son of a prophet"—I am neither master nor disciple in the institution of prophecy). Therefore, the truth of what the prophet says cannot be ascertained or measured by referring it to broad moral principles, the relevancy and cogency of which he may appear to be trying to "re-pristinate." *

b. The prophet has profoundly conservative impulses. He is aware that the divine will has been crystallized in institution. There are traditions that must be preserved and enhanced. Moreover, the prophet seems to have been tempted now and then to suppose that "in the old days it was better." So far, prophet and philosopher have not decisively parted company with each other. Divergence, if not settled opposition, appears when and where a determinative attitude toward tradition and social structure is revealed. *The prophet is preeminently concerned with reformation of the heart; the philosopher, so far as he is reformer at all, with the reconstitution of the outward structures of society and the inward structures of theory.* This does not mean that the prophet has

---

* This is acknowledged, perhaps inadvertently, in the Deuteronomic criteria for "true" as against "false" prophecy (cf. Deuteronomy 18:20-22).

no interest in structural changes or that the philosopher has no interest in motivations and intentions. What it means is that for the prophet the "heart" is so involved with social structure and with history that, unless its orientation is radically altered, ruination and death will put the final period to a sad and sordid story.

The distinctive aspects of the prophet's relation to institution and tradition come most fully to light at this point. In respect to institution and tradition, the prophet is neither conservative nor radical in the ordinary meanings of these terms. No general attitude toward these is possible for the prophet, because the decisive question about institution and tradition is: Are they, at a specific moment in history, effective expressions of the people's "memory" and the people's will to obedience? For the prophet there is no other really significant criterion for evaluating institutions and traditions, whether they are religious or secular. Does Israel remember that and how she is bound to the Holy God? Do cultic patterns and property-distribution arrangements, etc., express Israel's response to the demands of the All-Righteous Lord? If they fail here, their failure is absolute, unmitigated by any correlative or incidental value.

Someone other than the prophet could extract from such a view certain general and generally prescriptive principles. One could say, for instance, that commitment to and involvement in institution should never be absolute, because in that direction lie blindness and deafness to the living Word of God. Or again one could say that institutions themselves must be at once so simple and so flexible that they can be readily adapted to changing circumstances ("To your tents, O men of Israel!"). In a generously loose sense of the word, these attitudes might be styled "prophetic"; but the prophets do not seem to hold them. The reason for this is, if I may say so again, that the prophet does not for a minute suppose that critical apprehension of the human situation before God is available through a structure of theory. An "apperceptive mass" is required for the grasping of the word of God, yes; but the apperceptive mass is "memory," in which the mighty deeds of God in ages past live on. But memory is not all; the living God reveals the inner meaning of history now through the work of the prophet himself.

Eventually the prophet becomes a religious institution. As a phenomenon of religion he is flanked by legalistic moralist and by priest. Prophecy is assimilated into cult, and this cult is the heart of a culture. This route of assimilation cuts the root of culture transcendence, with-

out which prophecy does not live.* Thus the prophet as a critic of culture
has not been around for a very long time. But has not the prophet's
mantle been passed down to ready and willing heirs? The prophet no
longer thunders in our midst, but do we not hear prophetic voices? A
prophetic voice is one who cries out boldly against injustice in the social
order as a sin against God. A prophetic voice is one raised in protest
against the inhuman toll of massive institution. In general, these critics
of culture operate from the assumed truth of a philosophical-theological
point of view or system. The prophetic voice has (or someone whom
he trusts has) a conception of the good and of the human situation.
Moral judgments upon contemporary life are predicated upon the truth
and relevancy of this conception. Social protest may be the actual
starting-point of the prophetic voice, to be sure, and he may subse-
quently look about for theological justification for this protest. But so
far as a Protestant critique of culture is concerned, I believe it is generally true that social protest has been inspired by the adoption of a
theological viewpoint.†

The prophet has been succeeded by something rather more weighty
and perduring than prophetic voices. It is the church itself which has
a prophetic vocation, so far as any vocation can be traced as a historical
continuity to the prophets. The church does not license individuals to
be prophets; the church itself is prophet, so far as prophet is a religiously
significant term at all.

The prophetic vocation of the church—one of its God-given roles in
every society and every culture—is not the same as the will to be a
prophetic voice. This vocation is not fulfilled by drawing inferences
concerning the social order from a presupposed philosophical-theological doctrine. Judgment upon and about the social order is inspired by
its intuitions of the ground of human existence and of the world. This
ground is revealed in Jesus Christ, "through whom all things were

---

* Thus in the intertestamental period the "prophet" chides the people for their violations
of the law. He also serves as a morale booster in the days of fierce oppression, as he foretells
the imminent ruination of the heathen who so violently oppress the people. But the heart
of prophecy is now implicit confidence in truth and righteousness and wisdom once and
for all delivered unto the fathers.

† "Prophetic voice" is a term susceptible of malicious employment, as, for example, when
we use it to designate someone whose resentment of the comforts of others and their bland
enjoyment of these comforts is habitually disguised as moral judgment and who succeeds,
not in prying the favored few away from their treasures or vice versa, but in making their
enjoyment of same somewhat sour.

made" [see John 1:3; Colossians 1:16] and in whom the "fullness of God was pleased to dwell [Col. 1:19]." *

Like the prophet, the decisive attitude of the church toward social structures and orders is neither radical nor conservative in any ordinary sense of these terms. The ultimate question about any institution is whether and how it expresses man's relation to the authentic ground of his being, i.e., whether and how he is able through it to read positively the *intention* of his being as a creature of love. Thus, as in the case of the prophet, the criterion by which society is judged by the church is concrete. *This judgment upon society and culture is not ideologically determined.* Indeed, the church's ultimate critique of culture is not derived from any theoretical structure, not even (especially not!) from its own systematic or dogmatic doctrines. Its critique of culture is grounded in and expresses the *living* word.

It would be absurd to deny that the church's mouth is filled with all kinds of ideologically determined utterance. Say what we want about the church having a vocation higher than that of being a prophetic voice, does the church actually ever dream of being anything higher than this? Does it not refuse even this much as it scurries gracelessly for cover into its priestly office and its proliferous incidental ministries? Does not the church frequently, perhaps even habitually, vacate its prophetic vocation in order to become master oiler for the wheels of society?

Confronted by these questions, we are greatly tempted to take refuge in the venerable distinction between the ideal church and the actual church. The church *is* prophet: in the realm of pure ideality, untainted by dirty, intransigent fact. The church *is* a hollow reed which whistles and pipes with every ideological wind: in the realm of actuality, a realm perhaps illuminated but not disciplined by ideality. In our time particularly this temptation tugs at us with a vehemence and persistence we cheerfully call demonic. But so to identify the assailant is not enough. If the church is locked in struggle with more than flesh and blood, with "principalities and powers," no less, then it behooves the church to take up the full armor and arsenal of God! To put the matter in terms somewhat less exalted, the church must wipe from its glasses the mists

---

* I am assuming it is abundantly clear that we are concerned here with the church's understanding of itself. To report and interpret this self-understanding is part of the task of phenomenological description. Thus we are not assuming that what the church claims for itself is "really so."

of dubious metaphysics ("ideality versus brute fact") and have a fresh look at its actual existence.

In its actual existence the church cannot escape its prophetic vocation. Culture looks to it for a judgment, a critique, more fundamental than any other. Contending and contentious parties within society demand that the church's judgment should be fair, neutral, and spiritually edifying. These particular demands are almost always weapons in the power struggle, and they are calculated either to immobilize the church or to draw it into the support of one element in the internal tensions and conflicts of that society. The profounder demands of the culture are not always registered self-consciously and with high conceptual clarity. It is rather more likely that they will come to light in the arts and in the "psychopathology of everyday life." When culture is adrift, when it swings randomly in raging or becalmed seas of meaninglessness, the artist is the first to know it, or at any rate he is the first to put his intuitions into compelling form. But the "plain man" is rarely far behind him. The plain man cannot express his confusion, anxiety, and despair so dramatically as the artist, for he does not apprehend these conditions so vividly at the level of reflection. But the mood of the culture gets just as surely and as potently under his skin. If, therefore, the plain man comes to crave bread and circuses, it is not because the lords and masters first decided to provide these in order to corrupt and circumscribe his tastes and values.

The demand for a fundamental critique of culture is by no means a freak of our culture alone, artificially engendered and nourished by the priests and theologians. So far as any culture has come to be aware of itself (and I suppose that an unconscious culture is very nearly and for all practical purposes a contradiction in terms), it is aware of being related to what is beyond it. This means that culture and destiny are interlocked. Consciousness of destiny, in turn, is an *intentional* consciousness, i.e., it is a relating of spirit to being and world. This is precisely the point at which a culture expresses most clearly and more powerfully its demand for a critique that goes to the roots.

This demand comes all mixed up with other things. Who asks the naked question How am I doing relative to God's will? simply to add another item of information to his private collection, like a Clarence Budington Kelland hero? We all want to know not only where we are but whether we are "justified" in being there. In other words, consciousness of destiny is laced and riddled with anxiety. As a prophet the church speaks to this condition. And as prophet it cannot speak the word of false comfort and of illusory peace and self-justification without giving itself away.

Theology of culture is one expression of the church's vocation as prophet. This is an interpretation and critique of culture which is neither philosophy nor pure propheticism, but something of each and something beyond both.

Theology of culture is involved with philosophy and particularly with the philosophy of culture. In the philosopher, culture rises to its clearest (conceptual) "self-consciousness." It is the philosopher who asks the ultimate questions, not for himself alone but for his culture also. The ways in which these questions are asked reveal the heart of that culture. These questions must be answered as asked. Behind the philosopher's questions there are the structures of culture and, notably, theoretic structures (objective, not to be confused with the patterns of association of ideas in a given mind). If the church hopes to make a serious interpretation and critique of culture, someone within it must comprehend these structures and must be able to say what they reveal about life and spirit in that time and place. And these, clearly, are functions of the theologian.

Nevertheless, theology of culture is not philosophy. The theologian is licensed, as it were, by one institution within culture, the church, while the philosopher has a roving commission. This is not a question of truth and judgment compromised, if not corrupted, by institutional loyalties. On this score theologians do not come off conspicuously more poorly than philosophers. Rather, it is a question of whether one moves within a community in which being and truth are distinctively apprehended, that is, in a context where the mind of the thinker does not go the whole way on the basis of its own ontic intuitions but reposes an equal confidence in the memory and hope of the community. It may or may not be true that the mind always does this. The theologian is certain that his does.

There is a further differentiation of theology of culture: it must employ metacultural norms of judgment. The philosopher may do this also, or he may appear to do so. But the theologian has no choice; if he wanted the choice, he would have stepped beyond the "theological circle."

If theology of culture is not philosophy happily born in the odor of sanctity, it is not propheticism either. Propheticism is inextricably wedded to the futuristic tense so far as the kingdom of God is concerned.

God's judgment must be reckoned with in the present, but the kingdom is not-yet history. For Christian faith the kingdom has been revealed both to and in history. Therefore, the ontic ground of the human situation is symbolized not only as God the Father and God the Judge but also as God the Son and God the Spirit-Redeemer and Sustainer and Sanctifier. God so revealed demands of all men love for one another, not justice alone or primarily. Propheticism never reached this point. Its categorical policies stop with justice. And, incidentally, this seems also to be true of prophetic voices in the Protestant scene.

Furthermore, propheticism assumes the power for the renewal of spirit is somehow now resident within spirit; the wherewithal for repentance is implicit in the people of God. Christian faith makes no such assumption. Power for regeneration and transformation of culture comes in from beyond. This is the power of the kingdom now in history; but even though the kingdom is in history, it is still from God and of God.

Yet there is something of philosophy and of propheticism in theology of culture. *If the two had a natural aspiration for each other, theology of culture would be the point of meeting.* Theology shares with philosophy a concern for theoretic structures as instruments of analysis and as media of communication. With philosophy, theology of culture also shares a passion for universality of judgment (not to be confused with its impoverished cousin, the passion for absoluteness). There is also some agreement between them that the ills of a culture reflect or express constitutive problems of human life as such. So also propheticism lives on in the theology of culture. Propheticism is wholly wrapped up with the agony of the present. It makes no universal theoretic judgments. The God of all nations is not known as such by all nations; and his demands, his will, can be apprehended only so far as he makes himself known in a pinpointed present. This theme reappears in theology of culture: the will of God is known only so far as he reveals himself in and to a given people, a given community, at a given time. *That* God is, may be, and is known otherwise; but God so known is only the abstract possibility of judgment and redemption. God judging and God redeeming the present and ourselves in the present is apprehended only in the ontic intuition and in the life of faith projected therefrom.

But there is something in theology of culture derived neither from philosophy nor from propheticism, so that the theological enterprise in this realm is certainly more than a synthesis of the two. This "something more" is the common life, the community, established through Jesus Christ and continuous in history through the agency of the Holy Spirit.

Theoretic structures and ontic intuitions are here under the final discipline of historic event. This discipline is not mechanically and externally imposed upon the powers of ontic intuition. To the contrary the intuition is precisely the grasping of the ontic unity of ground and redemption.

Perhaps it is not necessary to say that this community does not function as a safe-and-certain refuge from which the theologian may survey the realm of culture. His vision is not blessed with supernatural correction for distortion and deficiency. His advantage is just that of believing that the living truth is in our midst, neither alien to our minds and spirits nor mastered and subjected by them.

Theology of culture is not to be understood as philosophy consecrated to the ends of religion and the church. It has philosophic strands; and upon occasion it is expressed in philosophic language; but as the tapestry is more than even its most beautiful strands, and a poem more than the words, so theology here is concerned absolutely with the Word of God, Jesus Christ.

Theology of culture is not to be understood as the theory demanded by a prophetic witness in culture, in order to give the witness honor and dignity in intellectualistic circles—a country parson sporting a D.D. when the summer crowd shows up. Theoretic structures and prophetic witness alike proceed out of the apprehension of God in Christ. True, theology must undergird the prophetic witness; but theology and that witness are sides of the same coin.

Theology of culture does not presuppose the truth of a metaphysical system. It does presuppose the pertinency of metaphysical questions. It is itself one formulation of answers to these questions. Just as answers to the question What is the good? are not properly deduced from answers to the question What is being? so here interpretation of culture is not properly deduced from answers to questions concerning ground, salvation, destiny. Rather, theology of culture is one mode in which these latter questions are answered. And therefore theology of culture is not God's answer to the prophetic voice praying for respectable theory.

Theology of culture is not to be understood as the church's pretentious answer to the pretension of the social sciences, any more than a course in biblical archaeology is a substitute for geology, paleontology, etc. The social sciences have their work to do. Those in charge of this work may need the prayers of the church, but they can hardly profit from specific spiritual instruction as to how they should do their work.

Moreover, while theology has a great deal to learn from these sciences, it has not to learn from them how to do its own work.

To sum up the matter positively: theology of culture is interpretation of a system of values, creations, and attitudes in the light of and on the basis of the revelation of being and good in Jesus Christ. The aim of such interpretation is very much more than to discover how far and in what ways a culture falls short of "Christian standards." The aim is to enable people of the church to discharge more adequately their responsibilities in the present moment. To "save the present age"; this is the aim. Where grace crowns genius, subsequent ages are enriched greatly by the theologian aspiring, above all, to serve his own age and his own people. Here, as everywhere, the saying is true and worthy of all acceptation:

> Who would speak for eternity and to all men has nothing to
> Say to me; But who speaks the word most revealing to me
> Carries the burden of eternity.

II

3
Living with Inevitability

Let us begin with a statement old-timers would consider psychological and more up-to-date types will recognize as existential. *The most pressing problem in the matter of inevitability is the practical one of living with the sense of it, whatever the objective realities might be.* So it is really about the sense of inevitability that I should like to spend all my time talking with you. But other aspects of the matter require some attention, even though what we really want is to get as much light as possible on the practical problem of living with a sense of inevitability.

Here, then, are the aspects of the problem I propose to deal with:

 I. There are some logical oddities in common uses of the concept of Inevitability.

 II. There are some oddities in our motives and interests in allowing the sense of inevitability to harden into theories and doctrines.

 III. The sense of inevitability is generally conveyed by images, the creatures and lords of imagination, rather than by doctrines or theories. We ought therefore to ask what might free the imagination and thereafter "mind and heart and soul and strength" from domination by the sense of inevitability.

 IV. There are some collateral issues; some of these are theological.

I

Let us begin by asking just what is being said when we say of something, "It was inevitable," since we commonly use the word in statements about the past. Here is an example of this.

Many years ago on a hot summer Sunday afternoon in the prairie country from which I came a very large cottonwood tree fell across a highway and pinned beneath it a car in which five people were traveling. Four of the passengers were killed outright and the fifth died later.

You can easily imagine the sorts of things we all said about the tragic and bizarre event. "The wind had to be blowing just right" (it was

53

blowing very hard), "The car had to be traveling at exactly the right speed," "But suppose the driver had insisted on having another cup of coffee at lunch that noon—just a couple of seconds either way would have spared them all," etc. Surely a neutral observer (the victims in fact were from elsewhere in the country and were strangers to all of us) would have objected to all this talk about the speed of the car and the velocity of the wind and the age of the tree all having had to be "just right." Would he not have asked, "Must not all the causal factors in *any* event be lined up just right to produce that effect for which they are the cause?" I doubt that any of us that Sunday afternoon would have rewarded that philosopher with anything but a blank stare, for we were drenched with the sense of inevitability. I for one thought that the incident deserved the talents of a Thornton Wilder; it was less exotic but fully as compelling as the story line of *The Bridge of San Luis Rey*. Here too was something that simply *had* to happen.

1. That common expression, "It *had* to happen," seems to be a fair substitute for inevitability. But now, when we say of something "It had to happen," do we suppose that there were events that did not *have* to happen though in fact they did happen? If we do not suppose this, what would be the point of saying of anything in particular that *it* had to happen, since by definition everything happens because it has to happen?

Odd as it may seem, there might be some point in making a distinction where we really ought to see one, and it is this: Some events are more heavily freighted with meaning—human meaning, of course— than others. To say of these events, some terrible, some sublime, that they *had* to happen is to remark their richness of meaning rather than to offer a differential causal explanation. But we would have to watch this differential meaning allocation carefully, very carefully; for we may unintentionally suggest that the governance of the cosmos aims at the production of value. That suggestion may quarrel fundamentally with the sense of inevitability. It is certain to quarrel with inevitabilist doctrines that systematically denigrate the scope of human intentionality even if they do not deny its meaning.

2. Inevitability is not intended just for the past. Perhaps you remember the Doris Day hit from the decade of the fifties, "Que Sera, Sera." In this opus Doris passes along the peerless wisdom of her mother: "What will be, will be." A fair translation of this doctrine might be: Whatever is to happen is sure to happen.

The natural question to ask, in the hope of obtaining further instruction from this doctrine, is, "But what will happen, more specifically? Is it to be A or B or perhaps Z?" No doubt you know that Doris' mother does not answer this question. But she is just as certain at the end of the song as she was at its beginning that whatever will be will be. Who will blame her for that?

So it turns out that what we are sure about in "Que Sera, Sera" is that whatever will happen is bound to happen. But did we ever doubt that? What indeed is there about that to doubt? We are not seriously tempted to suppose that some event in the future is going to fall between occurring and not-occurring.

3. It is unfair to take a concept or a doctrine at its worst. So let us acknowledge that talking about future events as inevitable may be a way of expressing a belief that the future is already determined. The fact that we do not determinate the content of the future does not count against that belief any more than our ignorance of past events implies that they did not happen.

So far so good. But this belief about future events offers the same double option that the inevitability of the past does: does it mean (a) that all events in the future are already determined or (b) that only the most meaningful future events are already determined? If we take (a), then of course we must be prepared to suggest why some but not all events in the future are already determined, for that determination can hardly be left to sheer chance.

4. Now we have stumbled over still another oddity in Inevitability. I cannot resist the temptation to chew on it a bit before discussing the most common of inevitabilist views of the future. I mean the oddity uncovered by asking the double question: At what point do future events become determined while still future, and who or what determines them?

In respect to the first part, we might say that what we call *future* is simply a human illusion behind which lurks a reality purely timeless. This is a fragment of ancient religion and metaphysics; many people still credit it. I don't suppose many of us do; we do not think about Eternity very much, and generally we don't know what to make of it when we do. In fact the powerful sense of inevitability is a testimony to our high if ambiguous regard for time.

In respect to the second part of the double question, the sense of inevitability predisposes us to believe that the determination of the future is out of our hands, no matter what the future may be, which is to say that "X is bound to happen" is the practical equivalent of

"There's nothing I can do about it." But then who or what is this mighty doer either of all things or of the things that matter most, the mighty doer whose power cannot be resisted? Religious tradition says *God.* The conventional forms in which this tradition now lives, if you can call it living, have largely stripped the concept of God of all rich explanatory and expressive power. Everyman's faith so far as this is revealed as Inevitability is in blind impersonal forces; these rule the future as they ruled the past; they are the real divinities.

5. Thus we come to Fatalism. In this view the determiners of destiny are indifferent to the general run of events. The general run may include decisions of finite free agents, beings such as ourselves. But the ultimate event is entirely out of human hands except for their unwitting instrumentality. So we are free to go to Khartoum or to Kankakee, to Teheran or Timbuctoo, to Sandusky or Samarra; but one cannot escape one's rendezvous with Death. Somewhere there is a bullet with your name on it, or a car bumper engraved with your epitaph, or a hyp needle with the germs assigned to your case, or a bolt of lightning prepared to ignore all other targets than you. There is no end to the imaginative particulars of the execution of Fate simply because there is an infinite variety of ways in which we can meet our Maker—or our Unmaker, if you prefer—but there is just and only one that is just the ticket for you, and you, and you; and for me, too, come to think of it.

The very commonness of these notions tends strongly to dim our awareness of how odd they are. Suppose, for instance, we ask who or what has put my terminal date in the cards. Only two answers are properly forthcoming to this question: (i) My terminal date is built into the system of reality, whatever we name it, "from the beginning." I put that last clause in quotation marks because it doesn't mean much of anything. How, that is, shall we say sensibly that the system of reality, the whole show, has had a beginning? In some religious traditions it makes some kind of sense to talk of the beginnings of the creaturely world. There is no way of talking sense about the beginnings of the whole show, God and created world alike. Moreover, that same devilish question comes at us again, now in this form: Is my sense of freedom in some of the things I feel and say and do entirely an illusion? If not, then those free acts, however minor and scarce, are not explained by appealing to the system of reality, unless we suppose that Reality is being made up as time rolls on. (ii) But suppose I decline, as graciously as possible, to be swallowed up by a system of reality and yet feel I must say that the ultimate event of my life, the paradox of my death, is eternally fixed, so to speak. Fixed where? Fixed in my nature, from which it seems to follow that I was born at a given date in order to die at a given date. But what sense does it make to say "in order to"? Certainly I cannot die unless I was born, but that is nothing like saying that to die is the reason I was born. It certainly wasn't my reason at the outset. I have never embraced it very warmly since, either. Then whose reason? Who gave me this nature? Do not say the genes did it. About those poor innocent little genes we must ask also: Were they born in order to die at a specific time? Why should we not say of them as well as of ourselves that their destiny is eternally fixed, not that they should just be bearers of our destinies but that each of them should have its own?

I suppose that we have all begun sometime since to wonder whether the *logical* necessity of coming to be at a particular time and ceasing to be at another particular time, since we are mortal beings, after all, hasn't nearly seduced us into trying to convert that kind of necessity into a kind of necessity far richer and far more desperate. I think that is the case. It is perfectly evident that since I shall die at some time it will have to be an entirely definite time, whether or not a grieving world takes exact note of it; but it does not follow that the definite time already exists, so to speak, somewhere or other. Indeed, such a notion makes no sense.

So we are so far entitled to this conclusion: As a doctrine, Inevitability either says nothing at all (what has been has been; what will be will be) or it promises far too much. But there is another complication to be introduced into the troubled life of the doctrine.

6. The *present* is fearfully jeopardized by the sense of inevitability; it is destroyed by the doctrine of the same name. This doesn't mean that the concept of the present is altogether easy. I suspect that is because the sense of it, the experience of it, is both so fundamental and transparent that the concept of the present has little left to do. If you are inclined to doubt this, or find it too wonderful either to be doubted or believed, consider the stark dependency of past and future on the present. Memory conveys a strong sense of Past and expectation a strong sense of Future. So far so good; but how far? Where is memory and in whom do expectations arise? Thomas Hood says:

> I remember, I remember
> The house where I was born.

Where lives that house but in the present act of remembering? Of course you might say, "Aha! I have you now. That house is still standing on the southeast corner of the intersection of Hilarity Avenue and Whimsy Lane. That's where the remembered house lives, if you want to call it living." I have only one comment to make about that, and that is that "still standing" means the present; and if somebody has to consult memory, or some other record, to make sure it is the very house the poet mentions, that too unavoidably acknowledges the present activities of one person or another. (I forbear to pursue the other possibility: namely, that the poet is speaking of the memory image and not about the "real" house "still standing.")

Another poet, Rilke, says that

> The future enters into us, in order to transform itself in us, long before
> it happens.

This tells us that the future cannot be said to be real in any honest sense unless there is some present being it can depend upon, some being it can enter into, in the poet's phrase.

Yet we must allow that one of the most puzzling and disconcerting experiences we have is the feeling that the present, however the sense of it, is trapped between the has-been and the not-yet, between the forever unchangeable and the essentially uncontrollable. What are we to make of this?

Well, we ought not to let anything dim the sense of the present, because it is the decisive experience of time. Indeed, even the sense of inevitability is a handle devised to grasp the import of the present rather than the past or the future as such. The past is something now happening to aspects of the world and the self. Future is something now happening to other aspects of self and world.

Obviously this does not mean that Caesar is just now being assassinated—though perhaps somewhere even now Shakespeare's play is being butchered anew. But it is the case that as soon as the image of the name of Julius Caesar comes to mind the past claims it; it is overcome, so to speak, by pastness. In fact, one of the more striking differences between the remote and the near past comes to light here: "Remoteness" signifies a virtually automatic sure-fire placement in the past; "nearness" shows that the present has not entirely relinquished the dead (whether person, occasion, or thing) to the past. Thus to entertain doubts or to manifest uncertainty about the deadness of Caesar is absurd; whereas nothing is more common or painful than to protest that the recently dead is not *really* dead. Of such a one we are very likely to say, "No, not dead! I can still feel the presence." Here we may be speaking of eerie feelings. On the other hand, what we really mean to say is that the present moment has not released the recently dead; we have the sense of occupying it with one whom in fact the past has claimed.

So it comes down to this: Inevitability is an incurably odd way in which the sense of time-present is stressed. In order to feel strongly that any part of time and the world is inevitable, we must have an even stronger sense of the present. But both the sense and the doctrine of Inevitability tend to obscure the boundaries of the present and to diminish its power. Why then do we accept these strange bequests of Inevitability?

II

Thus we come to the second objective of this chapter: namely, to ask what benefits we derive from Inevitability despite the oddities in our motives and interests in entertaining it.

1. One of these benefits is very similar to that obtained from any honest confession of helplessness: How can I be responsible for what cannot be helped? If we are all caught up in the toils of inexorable Necessity, why do we persist in blaming and praising one another? What happened had to happen. What is to be will be. How naturally we add the personal note: "I couldn't help it" and "There's nothing I (we) can do."

This is by no means a complete picture. There are some uncommonly strong people who embrace the doctrine of Inevitability, people who are not given to making excuses for failure to influence the course of human events. What do they find of benefit in Inevitability?

2. Strong minds as well as weak ones rejoice to believe that the world is absolutely orderly. If that is the way the world is, and human behavior too, despite the appearances, then it can be faithfully said of whatever happens that it has to happen—it is not one possibility among others fortuitously to be chosen by the world or one of its creatures. So if the world, including human history, goes in orderly fashion from one stage to the next, and from that next to another that grows out of it and so on to infinity (as well as from eternity), we can know where we are, and perhaps what, as well; though not necessarily why. So even if there is no overarching or pervasive purpose in the world, we ought to be able to make out the rational articulations of its successive moments.

3. Inevitability is also applied to the moral realm, with familiar and

remarkable results. (a) There is no escape from the consequences of wrongdoing, even though the innocent must reap some of the dire effects thereof. Better that the innocent should suffer than that the orderliness of the world should be abandoned! Here inevitability has become inexorability of moral judgment. The sense of moral responsibility ought to be elevated by this transformation. (b) Justice, peace, and brotherhood are certain to triumph in the long run. It may surprise some of you that people have looked upon these high goals of the human community as being quite as certain of eventual realization as proverbial death and taxes. In fact orthodox Marxism still does; therein the historical world runs toward a sure overcoming of everything that alienates man from himself and man from nature. What a faith! What a hope! What an odd and troubling thing that this theology of history makes so little of the image of man as the moral agent! (c) Marxism is not the only eschatological faith which views violent conflict and destruction as inevitabilities built into the structure of history, but it is now the most influential of such theologies. But again a goal of transcendent beauty lies beyond all the turmoil and suffering of history. In the meantime the most effective weapons of social control and of social aggression are justifiable adornments and legitimate instruments—in the hands of the Right Side.

4. Given such doctrines of Inevitability, the salvation of the individual consists in being on the right side of the sword of destiny. So even if there is nothing the individual can do on purpose to expedite (to say nothing of change) the development of historical reality, he can at least choose sides; he has, apparently, that much essential freedom. He cannot personally make a difference in the historical outcome; but his choice can make a very great difference in and for him.

It would be hard and profitless to deny that the sense of being caught up by the power which is shaping the fulfillment of human life altogether is a very wonderful thing. It is the sort of thing for which a person might sell his soul.

5. I do not believe that we can realistically and honestly deny that there are morbid attractions in the doctrine of Inevitability. For instance, to be powerless may well seem to be a rare blessing when power is ruining the world. There is also the perverse satisfaction in feeling that the worst is bound to happen, perhaps because one has predicted it. It is said that there are people in Hell who think they are really in Heaven because they are able all day long to say "I told you so" to people who can't escape them.

6. There is another function of Inevitability that we ought not to overlook now that we have mentioned prediction. That is a diminished or contingent application of the concept, such as, "X is inevitable unless. . . ." This has an interesting range of application: (i) "X is sure to happen unless someone has made an error in calculation." Logically this is very much like saying, "X is true unless it is false"; given a simple two-valued logic you can hardly beat either the truth or the triviality of that statement. (ii) "X is certain to happen unless the miraculous happens." This is not the same as (i); it is not matter of calling attention to possible errors in calculation; there is no way to calculate the occurrence of or the odds on a miracle. (iii) "X is certain to happen unless the people involved change their behavior, if not their minds and hearts." Such a change might be miraculous but there is a difference and it is important: Whatever our theories about the real and ultimate causes of human behavior, it is plainly true that some people are capable of changing; we know this because we do it and they do it; and we know that sometimes people change because they want to change.

The (iii) case illustrates the difference between the threat of doom and the promise of destruction. The weather does not promise a tornado. The God of the Old Testament prophets does not merely threaten.

Now, before we pass to the third objective of this outing, I want to put an intermediate question. Why doesn't the Doomsday strategy in human hands work? Is it because our attention span has grown steadily shorter and more fragile? As a people we do seem to be able to absorb if not digest crisis after crisis in and of society. They may not do us much good, but at least in our imagination they do not last long.

There is a more satisfactory answer to the intermediate question. It is a fact that the Doomsday strategy effectively closes down the options for a constructive moral-political response to grave dangers. Nothing could be farther from the intention or the divine authority of the true prophet. The picture of John the Baptist, for example, in the third chapter of the Gospel of Luke is that of a remarkably sane apocalyptic prophet. He preaches the early and violent end of the world with the coming of the kingdom of God. But he will not permit his hearers, thunderstruck though they are, to claim that the terrible vision paralyzes them. There is still time left to produce the "fruits of repentance": wrongs to correct, human relations to heal, life changes to carry out. We can well suppose that John's ethical prescriptions would have fallen flat and dead unless his hearers had grasped imaginatively the immense beauty of the kingdom of God, for one thing, and unless they had been given a positive rather than a negative motive for making the prescribed changes.

Today it is hard not to suppose that we are in a terrible race with time. But are we racing or are we rooted in one spot, frozen there by that peculiar and common anxiety called the sense of inevitability?

III

The sense of inevitability is generally conveyed and confirmed by images rather than by doctrines and theories. Images are the creatures and lords of the imagination. We ought therefore to ask what might free the imagination and thereafter the "mind and heart and soul and strength" from domination by the sense of inevitability.

The third part of this chapter is not at all intended to obliterate or obscure the morsel or two of reality buried in the sense of inevitability. Consider, for instance (i), that human life is indeed set down in a world of continuities. The future is a child of the past, up to a point. This is obviously true of human life if not for the whole world; which is to say that for so long as we live we shall continue to be what we have been. Popular beliefs in immortality reveal this in poignant ways. Taken together these beliefs powerfully suggest that the "other world" will find the souls of the blessed persisting in recognizable ways. Were it not so, most people would wonder what then would the point of Heaven be? If Heaven is not for this very self, why should I be for it?

Furthermore (ii), the sense of inevitability is closely related to the awareness that this life is not just what we make it. Our strength is too quickly spent and our lives with it. And we know just as surely that we are shaped by powers over which we have little control, no matter how much we learn about them. It is true that American society makes an adequate recognition of this most basic of facts difficult; the pressure is still on us to believe that the individual is a self-creator; so if he does not amount to much he has only himself to blame. But even in the glorious climax of the Work Ethic in Horatio Alger, there is an almost self-conscious recognition that Making It Big means getting on the Great Gravy Train. In less metaphorical terms, Success is a matter of learning how to relate to the vast, impersonal, implacable laws of the free market, the same being a shining model of an orderly (though hardly uniformly benign) universe. Thus the self-made man is not one who has actually conquered the world. He is precisely the one who has surrendered himself altogether to impersonal economic forces. In principle his decisions are tailored by the market; they are his only in the trivial sense in which the laws of motion were mastered by Sir Isaac Newton.

Thus in our time the conflict between the credo of radical individualism (the world is created for if not by the private ego) and the social reality of gigantic economic forces has surfaced dramatically. That credo does not let go of us easily. In fact it still commands many people whose hatred of the political-economic Establishment could hardly be enlarged or deepened. It is likely that this doctrine of the transcendent importance of the private ego has dictated a considerable range of efforts to create worlds, most of them fantastical, congenial to the value that private self is trying to protect against the massive denials of it looming on every horizon.

So another morsel of truth in Inevitability has come into view: We cannot wish or will away the continuities of time and the world; we do not have that kind of power. Anyway, much of the meaning of existence depends on them. There must be a world on whose regular behavior we can build.

Moreover (iii), we need protection of a spiritual order against the radical discontinuities of the world. We need to believe that the world is orderly, and we are gratified to find it so. But the world breaks out with raw contingencies, too; more than enough to go around. We have an arsenal full of defensive weapons for coping with the attacks of contingency. None of these is more trivial than the dictum: Learn to expect the unexpected. The thing is a logical contradiction. Worse than that, there is no way to do it. Of course we can practice to show no surprise when the unexpected strikes; but whom are we trying to impress, what game are we trying to play? When everybody else is saying, "My God! what do we do *now?*" I may be able to capture attention briefly by saying, "Well, I don't have any answer to that, but I can tell you I'm not really surprised to see that the heavens have fallen—you will remember that I have said all along this was bound to happen." I ought not to expect that the multitudes will be extravagantly grateful for this feat of self-congratulation.

A somewhat sturdier defense against brute contingencies is a sincere readiness to say of any untoward event, "It *had* to happen—it looks to be accidental, but really it had to happen." This is impressive because it is an effort to assimilate something apparently meaningless in its magnitude and power into a fabric of meaning. When we are able to do that, we feel that we have accomplished something important. Instinctively we feel that to understand even what we cannot begin to control is better than adding the insult of ignorance to the incurable injuries inflicted on us all by the great world. This is a strange instinct —and quite wonderful.

So there are morsels of truth in the sense of inevitability. The great practical problem is how to incorporate them into an outlook that does not take its marching orders from the sense of inevitability but yet accords it the justice it deserves.

The solution to this problem is to be found in the imagination, the great mother of the instruments by which human life in its concreteness is grasped and most powerfully expressed. More specifically, we need an image fit to rule over images in which powerlessness and nonresponsibility even for one's own life are expressed and vindicated.

This is quite a job. The images of vulnerability, of powerlessness alternately abject and proud, of bondage to blind fate, are all around us and within. They dominate much of the informal theology of the times—the popular arts and especially fiction and cinema. What then is easier or more natural than to construe our existence in the world as the plight of the Victim of the world? Hemingway's heroes are the victims of war, itself a metaphor of the blind brute contingencies of the world. Camus's people live in a world they never made (and who does not?) and are undone by its cruel, unintended decrees. How keenly he sees how fragile human happiness is! How shattering his sense that over every minute of happiness looms the shadow of the Executioner! Faulkner's people, except some of the Blacks, are doomed, and know it, by the gods of race and family honor; but even more surely and completely by their inability to close down the shops of memory. Over all of them looms the shadow of the Player, that wholly inscrutable Being who moves earthly creatures around to suit the requirements or the interests of a game known only to him.

Moreover, these images and sentiments of informal theology are powerfully reinforced by our perceptions of the actual situation in which history has landed us. The "neighborhood" cosmology was destroyed centuries ago, leaving man without a home in the natural world. The evolution of society in the Western world has repeated this disaster by creating huge concentrations of people and power, the modern city in which only its prisoners are able to feel at home: the people of the ghetto. They would not be the first to claim that urban society is a high achievement of creative community.

Our historical situation can be put in metaphorical terms: The modern world begins with the celebration of Prometheus, the Titanic hero who defied the high gods in bringing fire to earth. Thus Promethean man takes daringly his life into his own hands. He defies the gods of ancient servitude. He denies that he is accountable to a world other than his own. Modern man as Prometheus is the proudest of self-creators. But Prometheus is one of the Titans, gigantic in ambition as well as in size. Thus modern man has unwittingly created a Promethean society —one in which the Collective, the Corporation, aspires to engulf the whole human world—and now dreams of conquering the galaxy as well.

Now we see that the Corporation can only self-aggrandize at the expense of somebody or something. Something must become ever smaller if the Corporation is to become larger, and it is an eternal law that the Corporation shall become ever larger. So what becomes ever smaller? We all know the answer to that, but let us state it anyway: The zone of authentic self-autonomy becomes smaller and smaller. That seems to be an infallible perception of the situation.

So it is little to be wondered at that the images of Victim, Prisoner, Exile, and the like throng the imagination—and rule it. And that brings us full circle. *We perceive what the image dictates; we screen out what the image cannot* assimilate and control.

We need now to see as clearly as possible the implication of that. I take it to be that the imagination itself construes the field of action—life and the world—as a *player* would. The imagination plays with possibilities; and these run the full gamut from the horrible to the sublime, from the trivial to the ultimate. Indeed, even the most obdurate of "facts" is for the imagination a possibility, something to be moved hither and yon in the interests of evolving a pattern of meaning. That pattern is the object of the "play." What emerges from that playing may be fantastical, the gossamer of dreams. It may also be a "net" in which to capture and hold forever the real.

What then can we make of the images of player and game that will allow them to stand out against the fatalism of contemporary informal theology and yet will do justice to the heights and depths of the real world? Let us approach this by considering some of the prime features of game playing.

1. The world of the game is orderly; the order is the rules of the game. These rules are arbitrary but they are not irrational. Why does the batter have three strikes and four balls allotted to him rather than five strikes and seven balls? Why does the offensive team have four downs rather than three or five? The rules are arbitrary; they do not follow from the

eternal laws of reason, whatever those might be. But they define a particular game and there is nothing absurd about the game, though people sometimes advance absurd reasons for playing it. Moreover, the rationality of the game throws light on the irrational, such as changing the rules on whim, or to be sure of a win, or "losing one's head" and thus corrupting the game into a bloodfeud.

2. For the player the game is all-important for so long as he is playing it. That is, one doesn't really play a game for extrinsic purposes. If I do play a game for an extrinsic purpose, I have made that game part of some other game. A person who plays golf for his health wants to be healthy for the sake of some other game, such as his business or his profession.

But what about playing a game in order to win it? Isn't winning an ego gratification and isn't that extrinsic so far as the game is concerned, so far as play is concerned?

Both yes and no must be returned to the first question. It is true that one does not play, ordinarily, in order to lose. There are occasions when losing one sort of game is a move in another sort of game—a man may discover the value of losing the tennis match to his wife. On the other hand, a person who quit a game claiming that it was inconsistent with the intent and the rules of the game to lose it would be irrational, for it is part of the definition of some games that somebody must win and somebody must lose. It is, unhappily, true that winning a particular game or every game can become an obsession; this generally means the victim of that obsession is trying to prove something about himself which has little or nothing to do with that game or with any game he is playing at a given time.

So we say that the proper goal of the player is to master the game because it is in so doing (or in trying so to do) that the highest level of enjoyment is reached, win or lose. No wonder, then, that as spectators we love to watch two masters go to it, whatever the game, so far as we understand its goals and its rules. We know that somebody is going to win and the other party must lose. But that is the limit of inevitability. We know also that luck may well take a hand. But the way a master exploits luck is very different from the way of a duffer. The duffer prays for luck. The master designs to make some of the "breaks." A tennis player cannot get the break on a close call if he is incapable of putting the ball where he wants to. And simply to count on the breaks is both irrational and superstitious. The energy sacrificed to the goddess of Luck would be better expended in practicing the game.

3. Luck has nothing to do with mastering a game. To become a player good enough really to enjoy the effort requires systematic exercise of one's powers, both physical and mental, both imaginative and emotional. As the sportswriters like to say—and whatever they like to say, they like to say all the time—a master of the game is always thinking; but he is not thinking about the universe at large; rather, he is thinking ahead to the next move, he is figuring out what his opponent is up to, he is sizing things up rather than waiting for them to surprise him. And he knows that he must learn to keep his feelings in hand; he knows that his "attitude" must be right. These are not easily attainable goals. There is nothing automatic about acquiring them.

4. So training is indispensable to get the most out of a game. There is no serious play without it, any more than there is a game without rules. So if we begin by supposing that play is a natural element in human life, which is true, we ought also to see that good players are good because they put so much into it and because they know how to put their energies to the best use. Moreover, even a person with great natural endowments does not naturally become a good player. He becomes a good player only by unsparing discipline; that is, by an unnatural amount of hard work. For no one is it inevitable that he or she should master the game.

5. We are often and rightly impressed, nonetheless, with the *naturalness* of a great player, whatever the game. "He makes it look easy" is a spontaneous if somewhat misleading compliment to a great player. We know that what he is doing so flawlessly is not easy; we know that it does not just happen. The mastery of it may become "second nature"; it is certainly not first nature. Behind that artistry are uncounted hours of the most relentless application to technique, hours when mind and body alike cried aloud for "freedom of expression." Of course there is a paradox lurking just around that corner: The spontaneity that counts the most is available only after eternities of practice. Beethoven's improvisations at the piano were wonderful almost past belief. You would quickly find mine past endurance even as low comedy.

6. The performance of a master player is wonderfully reassuring to his audience, but not just because it makes us happy to see what a fellow human being can accomplish. The game is safe in his hands so long as he plays it—and so are we. Of course we admire his craftsmanship. Above all else we know that he can be trusted to take us where we want and need to go in and for that game, whatever it is.

IV

So much for some of the general features of the Player and the Game.
Let us try now to transfer some of the elements of Inevitability into this
context by asking these questions: Who is bound to win? What happens
when we see the whole of life in the world as a game? To whom does
that game belong? It is conceivable that some theological inferences may
show up as we consider this final run of questions.

1. In what has been said about the Player so far, we seem to have
assumed the eminence if not the sole authority of the adversary structure
in games; but not altogether, since we have also reviewed the play of
the artist for whom, ideally at any rate, competition is an extrinsic
though not necessarily trivial matter. Now it is necessary to correct the
assumption of the eminence of the adversary structure. Given an adversary Other in a game, it is inevitable that one side must lose and one
side must win (unless there are provisions for terminal ties). But suppose
that the adversary is an "ideal Other" rather than a flesh-and-blood
opponent. Suppose, in addition, that there is a very close relationship
between the playing self and the ideal Other; the player, that is, wants
above all else to improve upon his own performance, he wants to beat
his own record be it high or low, he wants to be better today than he
was yesterday even if there is no winner's crown involved. Of course,
he may still be seeking approval for his performance; but the plaudits
of the crowd may never be available to him, and they might not count
for much if they were. The crowd might have only a dim understanding
of the game, or it might not know what the stakes are. But the player
knows, and the ideal Other knows. Which is to say that the mature
player wants and needs the commendation of the ideal Other in any
case. The serious and wise player must play up to the limits of his
capabilities; when he does this he has a right to be proud. Conversely,
when he fails to do this he ought to be unhappy because he has let both
himself and the game down. There may be good explanations for his
failure—he may not have been feeling very well; he may have been
distracted by some woe of self or world. But the good player learns—and
the lesson is part of becoming a good player—to distinguish the good
excuses from the bad; in fact, he may well come to feel that if he is
able to go on at all then no excuse for a poor performance—one below
his capabilities—is viable.

Here it seems wise to pause and ponder briefly the remarkable ease
with which we submit to clichés about the good player. Consider one
going clear back to antiquity (my boyhood, in other words): "I'm

wounded, Coach, but let me play until I drop." And how about "My heart is breaking but the show must go on"? Or do you prefer "Better an honest defeat than a shabby victory"? In any case we can agree on "It isn't winning or losing that matters but how you play the game." Naturally there are beauties going the other way on the street where the Cliché lives, such as "Nice guys finish last" and "Winning isn't the important thing, it's the only thing."

What ought we to learn from even such a brief stroll on Cliché Boulevard? Surely that the image of the Player is vulnerable to corruption by false sentiment. The image can be absorbed into life systems in which both egoism and the destruction of the ego are avidly and dishonestly pursued. But these somber facts ought not to be given too much weight. Every game can be played for the wrong reasons, but that is just one detail of the general truth that every element and form of human life is vulnerable to corruption. Thus the adversary structure can be generalized to cover the whole of life and the world. This is a tragic corruption. It is not inevitable, even in a capitalistic culture.

2. It will seem to some that to see the whole of life as a game is sure to trivialize and cheapen it. That, undoubtedly, is a risk; again, however, it is not inevitable that we should fall into that trap. There are people who only "play at life" in whatever situation they find themselves; that is, they posture, they play up to the audience, they assume any role that promises to win attention if not applause, they change masks so swiftly and continuously that we seem never to see a real face. From such data we are likely to conclude that the realities of self and world for such people have simply evaporated. We want desperately to say to them, "For God's sake quit *acting* and try to *be!*"

On the other hand we have all had some experience with people whose lives as a whole are infected with a deadly virus of self-seriousness. When these people say of others, "So-and-so is altogether too light-hearted, oh so terribly lacking in seriousness!" we strongly suspect that they have themselves in mind as models of unblinking recognition of the harsh realities of life and of relentless dedication to the ultimate good. These are the people who cannot afford the time or the energy to laugh; they have postponed that to heaven and feel that they don't need any practice in this life.

The proper image of the Player calls into judgment both ends of this spectrum. The true player knows that life in the real world is something to be enjoyed; it is something to receive, to pursue, and in the end to hand back, with joy. This kind of lightheartedness has no room for callousness or blithe indifference to the presence of evil of any sort. Callousness is either a natural or a cultivated insensitivity to some threat of evil in existence. The true player does not need and cannot use that sort of defensive weapon. Risking a cliché, let us say of him that he wants to "play the ball where it lies"; that is, he wants and needs to learn what of good can be made of any and every situation. So the true player does not know and does not ask to know how he will fare in harsh adversity. What he wants to do and prays for grace to do is to "play up"; that is, to do the best he can and leave to God the outcome. There is a sort of blitheness in that, a sort that has nothing to do with indifference.

3. "Leaving the outcome to God" does not necessarily bespeak a strong religious position. It may be a cliché used to express, and also partly to conceal, an incurable human limitation: We cannot control the future. "Leaving the outcome to God" on the other hand may express a deep religious conviction: The game as such, as a whole, belongs to God; he preeminently is the Player. Thus the ancient confession, "The world is his and he made it," can be construed as a hint that God's relationship to the world is very weakly conceived and practiced as that of a handcrafter to his product. A game is only incidentally a product, an artifact. We can of course say of any game that it is a product of the imagination, but it is not really a product; it is, rather, a set of directions for the expression of energy in maximally enjoyable ways. But above all a game is a specification for confrontation between creative selves and ideal demands. The rules of the game signify some of those demands; their definiteness is a sign both of indispensability and of relatively low value. The rules define an "economy"—they are housekeeping principles. But the essence of the game is the outlay of physical and spiritual resources to achieve one kind or another of human excellence. Within the rules there is no limit to what one can undertake to achieve that; the rules do not specify how long one is to practice or with what devotion. We are not free to break the rules; within the rules, we are free to make of ourselves the sorts of players we want to be, but not absolutely free because each of us starts from one condition rather than another. I am not and am sure I never was free to make a Bach of myself. At one time I was free to learn to play Bach with some artistry and authenticity. I am still free to enjoy him. "Bach" thus is not the name of one of God's products. Bach is one of God's immortally great players. God played—not toyed—with him; and he with God. I thank them both for allowing me to play their game, that "joy of all desiring."

If God is himself above all else the Player and not just the owner of the game, then certain types of religious bets are far off the mark—and above all the others, that sort of outlook and piety that denies to mankind, to human beings, any real role in the determination of human destiny. True, if God is the Player supreme, we cannot hope to beat him at his own game; but why should we want to do that? That is the question to which Milton's Satan—the greatest of that fiendish crown —has not the slightest shred of plausible answer. For if God has called me to play out a life in relation to him as the supreme contestant, as the transcendent Other, then I know that the game matters infinitely and I am incited to dream, perchance to plan, an infinite enjoyment of it. It will go (it has gone) against me, no doubt about that; but he will not throw me out of it, he will not disbar me or rule me ineligible, so long as I am human.

At this moment in our history there is nothing in the least inevitable about believing such things. It is a plain if not simple fact that ever so many people do not believe them, and it is equally plain (if far from simple) that some of these people say it is inevitable that we shall all give up believing these religious things. But that is all right; it is all all right. About all the things that greatly matter there ought to be something optional. To be sure, life is commitment and all that. After commitment, not before it, the real game begins. So of course I believe, and commend to you, the proposition that for God too the fun begins with and after "the creation of the world." That was when "the morning stars sung together for joy." No doubt "fun" offends some of us—what's so funny about the cross? I assure you I use "fun" innocently to suggest that for God transcendently enjoyment is the "name of the game." This does not mean that in heaven there is the slightest trace of blithe indifference to human suffering. For the Christian the cross signifies an enjoyment that freely embraces tragedy but is not defined by it, and thus a truly and absolutely divine power to love that will never rest until "sorrow and sighing have been banished forever and there is no more night."

So I believe that part of the game of God is to endow human beings with the miraculous potentiality for "giving thanks in and for all things." That means both for the things that can be changed and the things that cannot. There is in us the capacity for making an appropriate response to each kind of thing. That too is part of the game.

Inevitabilism of any brand has only a very slight place for thanksgiving except for ceremonial purposes or otherwise as a kind of duty. There is no joy in that; or if there is, it is accidental. Well, if a person feels that the world is a trap with hardly any choices at all but in what minor key to sing its wretchedness, he is not likely to enter its courts with joy. Thank God there are other ways open to view life in the world and other ways of singing. At the moment it is far more important that we should all see that this is the case than that we should all thank my God. If you do see this, I will happily thank him for you.

4
Encounter and Inference in Our Awareness of God

The topic I have chosen for this chapter may have confirmed a widely held conviction that some theologians manage to miss the existential flavors of their times by a small margin and the rest by a large margin. "Encounter and inference" indeed! Surely the times cry out for candid confession that the collapse of the traditional structure of belief has brought down the traditional *problematic* as well. Standing honestly in the middle of this scene, we might then assay the incantations and imprecations of new pieties that fill the air. Instead of that, I seem to be proposing an exercise in logic. The religiously concerned will hardly find comfort in the fact that the exercise is a very primitive one, for why bother with that sort of thing at all when the crisis of church and culture is so severe? Logic never lifted a soul to God or brought heaven to earth. Why then wander on the cold, arid, and infertile plateaus of logic while here below the multitudes hunger desperately and thrash about frantically for a meaningful existence?

What is worse, I am not a logician of high technical competence. Thus to the melancholy generalization that theologians past thirty have a habit of getting to the scene after the action has shifted elsewhere, it may be necessary to add the judgment that this one arrived with a gun one end of which he couldn't tell from the other. Need I add that self-destruction has a 50-percent probability in that case?

I must, accordingly, now make one thing clear: This is not an exercise in logic. My purpose in this chapter is to offer an account of the way a certain vivid religious experience can be related to certain elements in the structure of Christian belief. What I have in mind by "vivid religious experience" is the prophetic encounter with the living God in

This chapter is reprinted with permission from *The God Experience*, edited by Benjamin Whelan. Copyright © 1971 by The Missionary Society of St. Paul the Apostle in the State of New York.

the maelstrom of social revolution. What I have in mind by "the structure of Christian belief" is a body of teachings in which God is the capital item, the beginning and the end.

The central thesis of this chapter could, then, be expressed in a somewhat more argumentative way. The prophetic encounter with God makes arbitrary demands upon the structure of Christian belief, and making the most of this encounter requires the development and employment of routes of inference (or inference patterns). The fact—as I take it to be—that prophets are impatient with inferences and preoccupied with encounters serves to remind us that there is and must be more to Christianity than prophecy. The prophet, in fact, does not add to our knowledge of God. He may bring to us a fresh recognition of our actual situation in the sight of God. That is a great, dangerous, and painful thing to accomplish: painful for us, dangerous for him, great with the possibilities for the reconstruction of the service of God.

It will become evident in what follows that I am using "prophetic encounter" to designate a current religious phenomenon rather than an institution in ancient Israel or an office in the early church. Thus the contemporary Christian prophet demands that we go out from bastions of power and privilege to encounter God where he is to be found, in the center of the revolution, and there to do his bidding, on which the prophet claims to have explicit information.

The prophetic spirit in our times does not make much of other encounters with God. I do not find that this is commonly a theological decision made as such. It is a result of personal stress and of social urgency. From a generic Christian belief that God is encountered everywhere, the prophet extracts and specializes the inevitability of encountering the God of utter righteousness. He seems therefore to avoid the embarrassments which cluster around the traditional belief that God is encountered everywhere, could we but recognize him in all things. For so soon as we say God is that being we cannot avoid, we are asked, "Why call that being 'God,' to say nothing of 'the God and Father of our Lord Jesus Christ?'" For death is also something we cannot avoid, in any case. So is guilt. And taxes. And conflict. And sex—I hope. Christians are rather notoriously reluctant to call any of these inevitabilities "God." Yet Christians have been rather notoriously prone to claim that God has a hand, and the winning hand at that, in all—repeat, all—creaturely inevitabilities. How, then, can Christians gracefully decline to answer such a question as, "Why do you not say that Death is one of the names of God? You say that God is somehow implicated in death; but you insist that he is Life rather than Death." And so also for Sex. D. H. Lawrence strove with rare dedication to convince our parents that sexuality *is* a "name of God." Was it just prudishness that made them shy away from that passionate avowal? Perhaps. But they have also believed that while the right enjoyment of sexuality might well be praise of God, sex as such is not a route of access to him.

The general theological situation of the Christian belief in God seems to be an angular logical oddity. God is honored as the creator of all things—death, guilt, taxes, war, sexuality, whatever. He has not done all things in the same way, but in all things his doings can be made out, somehow. But he *is* not anything he has made or done. The name of nothing in creation can be ascribed to him. Yet there is a way of reflecting upon the eventualities of life, and upon the sheer existence of whatever exists, that is a route of access to God.

I think it could be shown that even the hardiest "revelationist" in recent Protestant theology makes his own awkward admissions of this logical oddity, however ferociously the fans of his theological windmill assail that Don Quixote, Natural Theology. But let us not suppose that any of us gains by perfecting the spread of theological embarrassments. It is more important to learn whether the prophet has a way out of this logical mess; and specifically, whether the encounter with God in the center of social revolution is such as to absolve prophetic religiousness from responsibility for showing just what is divine (or God) among the multifarious powers working the dissolution and reconstruction of the social order.

II

I propose to attack this issue, and the larger or more encompassing logical oddity, by reviewing the classical structures of inference.

1. Something exists: therefore, God.
2. Something is going on: therefore, God.

Now let us dress each out a bit.

1. From the fact that anything exists ("anything" being the blank check for something particular, determinate, finite), it follows that the proposition "God exists" is a true proposition. Or, in the most abstract terms, *"finite" implies "infinite."*

The second structure (2) can be rendered in at least two different ways.

a. The world is made up of processes all of which start and eventually stop. Yet the world does not start and stop. Hence *change* implies *permanence,* which, spelled with a capital P, is God.

b. Something is happening so momentous that it must be God's direct doing. How can God do something *directly* without being *present?* How can he be present without being present somewhere and to somebody?

(a) and (b) seem to have nothing to do with each other. (a) reflects a cosmological concern like (1); and (b) a revolutionary historical one. (a) seems to aim at the validation of a cosmological proposition. (b) seems to aim at the recognition of a Presence—a power perceptibly at work in our history and existence.

The cosmological route (1 and 2a) has been in acute disfavor in Protestant theology for well over a quarter of a century. Apparently this state of mind is now well established in Catholic centers, too. Quite apart from the fact that it is a blatant expression of confidence in human reason (cognitive powers) there is a greater embarrassment: There seems to be no valid and instructive way to get from Principle of Permanence to "the God and Father of our Lord Jesus Christ," or from beings to Being. This difficulty can be rephrased. *Whatever avails to render experience intelligible (here the experience of change) does not necessarily expose anything salvific or properly divine.*

It may be that these charges rest upon a serious misunderstanding of the cosmological structures of inference. Were they designed to carry the mind from "intelligibility" to "savior" or "salvation"? Were they supposed to be the launching platform for the ascent of the mind from the general features of experience rightly understood to God Almighty rightly worshiped? Is it not rather the case that "Change implies permanence" only when it has been antecedently determined that change of itself is unintelligible? Many defenders of the cosmological route have indeed operated from that antecedent determination. Or, again, "Things are happening" implies "There is a Source of all action" only when it has been antecedently determined that the preeminent model of "Something is happening" is a conscious volitional subject producing or generating action. Again, many—probably most—followers of the cosmological route have operated from that antecedent determination.

The real inferential structure of the cosmological theists seems then to have been this. Appeal to the data of experience is logically a display of the explanatory capabilities of theistic belief rather than the first step in the rational construction of that belief or the kingpin in its validation. Thus the experience of change, contingency transitoriness, etc., is an encounter with God himself. This encounter is not a direct, unmediated awareness of God as the supreme subject from whom all things come. It is, rather, an awareness of being caught up in something God himself must be doing; that is, *evaluating change as well as causing it*. This does not mean that God must ask what we must often enough ask—namely, "What is going on here?"—before we can rationally proceed to appraising it. Let us say, rather, that the "power of God unto salvation" presupposes a judgment on God's part that things are not what they ought to be. Thus the cosmological structure of inference is not as remote and alien to the historical inferential route as many theologians seem to suppose.

Nonetheless, (2b) is obstensibly a revolutionary-historical concern rather than anything even remotely cosmological. "Something so momentous is happening that it must be God's direct personal doing. Properly focused and refined perception is able (or ought to be able) to discern God as present in the determination of these great events." It must therefore seem uncommonly high-handed to say, right off the bat, that there *is* an inferential structure embedded in this encounter with him whence comes the "permanent revolution." But I think that is the case. For what is actually *encountered?*

Powers destroying the old world and powers shaping a new and, it is hoped, a better one. The claim of (2a) is that God is present among them, and that is where he can be known. Indeed, (2a) contends that unless we meet him there we are not going to know him as he really is, at all.

Nothing could be farther from my intention than to minimize the ethical passion evident in this claim. It is a timely and powerful rebuke to religious strategies for private salvation. When there is a world to be won or lost, how could a really moral person wish to be plucked as a brand from the burning? Surely, in this historical moment a retreat to ethical and religious privacy is *eo ipso* a flight from God! If God can be encountered only where "cross the crowded ways of life," it is folly, if not heresy, to suppose that he can be encountered in private, self-interested worship—or, we may add, in sanctuaries soundproofed against the mounting war of a world in violent upheaval.

Let us agree, then, that the issue is not ethical authenticity. The issue is theological. How is God recognized as *God* in this world of revolutionary upheaval? Is he the true author of revolution, his breath the whirlwind beating against the walls of alienation, the structures of injustice, until they come tumbling down? Or is this rise and fall of empire a rhythm God built into the human commonwealth, there to stay so long as man lives on earth?

These are not the only theological options, but they are the ones which stand in the sharpest contrast to each other. They are also the ones which typify in our time the perennial opposition of Intuition and Inference, in the Christian's knowledge of God. We are therefore justified in devoting careful attention to this contrast.

III

If I say that God is only to be encountered where the revolutionary action is, I ought to brace for the natural and inevitable question: How do you recognize *God* in the general turbulence? Since we have agreed to put aside private visions and every other kind of subjective assurance, I should have to say one of two things.

1. What I *mean* by "God" is a being who is dedicated to destroying injustice in order that the light of love and peace may break out across the human scene in uncorruptible splendor. Consequently, wherever I find human beings so dedicated and so energized, I say, "This is God's work" and "Here God is present." From this it is but a short step to the acknowledgment that "God" is a name for the noblest and most fertile human passions. "God" is the concert of passions focused upon the perfection of the human commonwealth. And surely *this* God is encountered in every such passion and every such concert. About that there should be no theological mystery at all.

The mystery sets in at another point: Why use "god language" at all, if that is the upshot? Is it an accident, a mere coincidence, that the ideological masters and architects of the most massive political revolutions in the modern world have been avowed atheists? No doubt atheism is often a rejection of the church as an institution rather than as a systematic metaphysical view, and a criticism of its behavior rather than of its beliefs. But surely part of the meaning of the slogan "the world coming of age" is just the conviction that what man has messed up in his own affairs he can and he must straighten out by himself.

Still, if it were simply or largely a semantic decision involved here, our theological worries would indeed be few and miniscule—a matter, that is, of what name to supply to the absolute to which one appeals as the ultimate justification for one's revolutionary posture and practice; for then where I say "God" you might say "the historical dialectic" and someone else, "the ultimate ethical commonwealth," etc.

But this is not simply a semantic decision. Whether or not the philosophers give their approval to such habits, we do habitually suppose that the use of the word "God" infers it is serious, puts us into a reality-game and not just into a language-game. Why would I appeal

to the manifest will of God as the ultimate justification for some principle or policy if I were persuaded that *this* God does not exist, is not *there*
to have and make known a righteous will? Assuredly, if I believe God
endorses some principle or policy to which I am attached, this attachment is likely to be strengthened thereby; but only so far as I hold that
the belief is sound. My conviction that I ought to do my duty would
hardly be strengthened by my believing that the ghost of Kant nods
approval. For even if I believed that ghosts exist and that Kant might
well be hanging in there, I should still be dealing with a morally fallible
being (I hope that the ghost of Kant is not offended by that remark);
and I cannot and do not appeal to such, living or dead, as an *ultimate*
justification for principle or policy.

We have now to return to the question to which so far only one kind
of answer, and that an unsatisfactory one, has been returned, namely:
How does one recognize *God* in the turbulence of historical crisis?

2. To this it must seem far more satisfactory to say that God can be
counted on to make himself known, and never or nowhere more clearly
than when the human stakes are the highest; that is, when the human
commonwealth is most powerfully threatened.

We have two good reasons for looking into this viewpoint. The first
is the ethical seriousness of the prophets of social revolution. The second
is the formidable difficulties which the notion of the self-authenticating
character of divine revelation encounters.

IV

Let us agree that the most interesting form of the inferential structure
sketched above is this: "Something so momentous is happening that it
must be God's direct doing. Properly focused and refined perception
is able to discern God as *present* in the revolution of our history." Thus
to know him as he is we must know where he is. In that encounter alone
will come the holy shock of recognition.

Something like this is the gist of the theology of contemporary Christian prophecy. Within this striking religious formation I make out two
quite different ways in which recognition of God is claimed, which I
shall simply call Type A and Type B.

Type A. *The prophet recognizes the hand of God in history; and not
merely in the history of the "almost chosen people."* As Amos long ago
saw, the hand of the Lord is raised against injustice and cruelty wherever
these monstrous enemies appear on earth. The Lord will not stay the
rod of punishment whether the culprit is Israel, Judah, or Syria, etc.

Assyria comes down from the north like a ravening wolf to devour faithless Israel, but Assyria also is destroyed for her own iniquities.

This prophetic message can be formulated in more general and philosophical terms. The result will sound something like this: Every society feels the pressure of Ideality, and specifically the pressure from the ideals of Justice, Freedom, and Peace. And every society responds in its own way to these pressures. The builders and defenders of an empire know in their bones that Fortune has presided over its birth and that the president deity keeps a jealous eye on the performance of its darling. Thus even empires must hew to a line of rectitude (however primitive this seems to the prophet) or suffer the awful consequence. This much Tacitus saw and proclaimed even while Rome was rising to dizzy heights of power and glory. Eternal Rome indeed! He knew that the germs of destruction and death were already at work.

The prophet of the one true God has a broader vision. He recognizes the hand of God in the rise and fall of any and every empire. The prophet discerns a rhythm, a law, in human history. Imagination, fired by evil appetite, conjures an empire in which the many live for the advantage of the few. Given a break here and there, the evil dream comes true and the happy few may for a while rule the multitudes of the world; but only for a while. The regnum may seem to run forever, but this is an illusion.

It takes a prophet to recognize the arm of the all-righteous Lord in the destruction of empire. What meets the unprophetic eye is the destructive impact of the appetites of people who want more and more of the goodies for themselves, and the diminishing concern for justice and mercy. Or the superior might of another empire bent upon "synthesizing" weaker achievements often accounts for the fall of the one and the aggrandizement of the other. It takes more than the naked eye to recognize a higher justice in that. But the prophet has an answer to these sour generalizations. He claims that God uses the fallible and corrupt powers of man to work the ultimate design of justice, peace, and freedom. The prophet speaks for the righteous God who reigns supreme over the rhythm of empire.

No matter how stirring the performance of the prophet of this persuasion, we are beset by theological problems when we come home from the show. The Christian moralist knows what to think of a *human* agent who deliberately employs or piously ordains the use of evil instruments to achieve a good purpose. Is a presumptively divine Agent *rationally* immune to that condemnation? Moreover, the God who reigns supreme over the rhythms of empire is remote from the dreadful struggles which rend the human commonwealth. So where is the virtue in saying that *in the end* his will prevails? For we have no way of getting at (either to know or to correct) the vision of the end such a God might have, if indeed the "end" of the historical process (the rhythm of empire) is in anything different from the process itself. Through his prophets this God teaches us that injustice does not pay. But history teaches us that making the unjust pay up is an atrociously expensive business, and count the expense in any terms you want. The mills of the gods grind slowly. They also chew up a lot of innocent people. To reply that none is innocent cheapens the whole game.

We should expect a *Christian* prophet to recoil from these inferences. We should expect—to put it somewhat more affirmatively—the Christian prophet to hold out for a divine intervention in the process of history. For how can he be Christian (if that connotes anything but idealism) if he does not believe and preach that God is really present in the ongoing struggle to deliver the human commonwealth from its besetting evils? So far as we are Christian we expect God to do something more and better than to preside over history. We expect him to be really present in it, in order to make sure that one day his creation will become what he intends all along that it should be.

Thus we are brought to Type B, the prophecy which recognizes God as the supreme eschatological Presence in the great crises of history and thus in the revolution which has seized our life.

Type B. Here the mode of recognition of God appears to be largely intuitive; that is, a direct apprehension of a present reality. The prophetic consciousness, Type B, apprehends God present here and now. God is the sublime eschatological Presence, he who shapes the future for the perfection of the human community and who does this divine work from within the perimeters of the human community.

I think something like this lies behind the burning conviction that one can encounter God only where the action is. This is the commanding prophetic passion of the hour, and it seems to put its subjects in much closer communication with the revolutionary spirits outside the church and the faith than with the defenders of tradition. "God has moved outside the church" is a sentiment heard frequently in the church itself. It is often expressed with such earnestness and singlemindedness that one is reluctant to do anything to modify the passion, such as saying that even the doughtiest defender of the ancient doctrine that outside the church there is no salvation would never have dreamed of denying that *God* is "outside the church." The God of the Tradition is hardly a household deity, even for the household of faith.

Nevertheless, the work of theology is not all passion, not even the most admirable passion. It does, I am afraid, require us to ask disconcerting questions, such as: How do you know it is *God* you encounter where the action is? Type B prophecy is very likely to say, in response, something like this: "When you do God's work out there on the action front you just *know* God is present. It is almost as though we can *sense* him as we are drawn up into the battle to deliver men from the fetters of injustice, slavery, war, hatred, etc." What can we make of this? Several things.

1. It has a certain mystical air about it. Almost every kind of religious life promises some kind or degree of community with the Ultimate, provided that the person who seeks this is prepared to accept the discipline of a community. Granted that the prophet in our days is likely to minimize the values of the traditional cultic community in order to elevate the company of people who have been "out there" together. In that company one senses the magnitude of the revolutionary task; and one senses, from time to time, a sublime Presence permeating that company, healing the wounds inflicted by the outer world, and overcoming the alienations which develop in any human society, no matter how noble its purpose and how dedicated its members.

2. But another interpretation comes to mind. The prophet recognizes God in the revolutionary confrontation because he knows that this is the sort of thing God would be interested in, to put it somewhat whimsically. Properly instructed by Judaism, Christianity teaches that God is righteous altogether. If we are to serve him properly, therefore, we must make every effort to straighten out whatever is crooked in our life and our world. It is not enough to be sorry. It is not enough to insist that injustice is as old as the human story and that every reform brings in new evils. God still demands that we "bring forth fruits worthy of repentance." The first Christian cells laid great stress on the life of love within their perimeters but did not intentionally paper over inequities with amiable sentiments. Yet they did not grasp the immensity of the eschatological Presence. Nor, for that matter, did they dream that one day the church would feel obliged to accept the reigns of government from the dying hands of the mightiest of imperial states. The religious and ethical mentality apparent in the Apocalypse of St. John is hardly compatible with the assumption of civil governance; and so the former yielded to the necessities of the latter, and the church became an empire among the other kingdoms of this world.

God as the eschatological Presence was not defeated by this worldly triumph. He moved out and on, not so much to bring down an imperialistic church as to build up responsiveness to his real presence elsewhere. Eventually the imperialistic church came down—or should we say it is still coming down? The point is, it did not come down through the operation of some "law of history." It came down because the Creative Spirit had gone off and left it.

3. Type B prophecy makes much less of *law* in history and much more of the *contingency* of history. The God recognized in the revolutionary upheaval is not the God who presides over the rise and fall of empire. Rather, he is God always present to release the victims of every captivity, ancient and modern. He is on the side of essential freedom. Indeed, he *is* the spirit of essential freedom. As such he cannot have an ultimate regard for Law; it is not at the top of his priorities. Thus Type B prophecy is much inclined to treat law and rule as human conventions rather than as divine arrangements, except so far as freedom and love might be spoken of as lawlike, e.g., "I give you no law except that you should love one another." It is, I suppose, clear that this is much more like an ethical norm than a law; that is, it is a nonenforceable prescription.

If this account of Type B prophecy is reasonably correct, then it would be hardly consistent with it to speak of a divine *intervention* in human history in behalf of justice, mercy, peace, brotherhood, etc. "Intervention" still carries too much of the scent of "miracle," the event that suspends momentarily the laws of nature. This conception of miracle gives away far too much weight to the reign of law, either in nature or history or both. So where essential freedom is given the highest priority, law ought to be regarded as somehow derivative from freedom.

Thus God as the ultimate supreme Revolutionary does not have to struggle against any legalistic factor in his own makeup. He is the eschatological Presence inspiring and perhaps directing the demolition of institutions and sanctions that alienate man from the brother. God is absolutely free to seek the release of human creativity from whatever obstructs, obscures, or diminishes it.

We have, thereafter, only two questions to put to his prophets. One: Is this God also proportionately powerful to enforce his holy will? Two: How does the man of faith distinguish *God* from worldly powers *accidentally* creative-constructive even though they are essentially either destructive or "value-free"?

The two questions are intertwined. If God is identified with the powers undermining the massive institutions of our civilization and their theological-ethical sanctions, God emerges with just so much power and resourcefulness as revolutionary forces in fact display, unless we are given some theological grounds for believing that the eschatological Presence is holding vast powers in reserve for the moment he has ordained for their deployment. Type B prophet has not yet come forward with those theological grounds. But from this some fairly curious results flow. For one, a defeat for the Revolution becomes *eo ipso* a defeat of God—not a defeat *for* God but a defeat *of* God. It is not entirely clear that this is the sort of thing Paul had in mind in speaking of the "weakness" of God (1 Corinthians 1). And there is another inference: If revolutionary forces succeed only in disrupting the social order, and nothing constructive emerges or even promises to emerge, God, so far as he is identified with this revolution, seems much closer to Death than to Life, to the shedding of blood rather than to concord, peace, and love.

We can have no doubt that the Christian prophet is made very restless by this sort of discussion and would move to end it with some such claims as the following:

"But of course as *Christians* we know that God is entirely on the side of love, justice, and peace. He *cannot* be identified with anything merely destructive, hateful, and anarchical. Nor can he be identified with any 'value-free' social process. In the turbulence and tumult of the present hour, God is the spirit of love leading the faithful to seek justice for all by the appropriate methods of social criticism and social reconstruction." From this it would seem to follow that the faithful Christian might not applaud the destruction of the social fabric but might yet see in this process something providential; namely, an opportunity to make the case, existentially if not theologically, for self-sacrificial creative love.

Be that as it may, we have still to decide whether the Type B Christian prophet is fundamentally and decisively committed to a kind of intuitionism in his claims to have recognized God in the scene of turbulent social change. I think he is, unless he is now prepared to admit that what he calls "recognition of God" *is actually a way of claiming part of the structure of Christian belief to serve as a sanction or warrant for his way of leading the Christian life in the world.* If this is the case, we have left intuitionism far behind for any purpose other than a method for grasping a critical situation as genuinely critical. Thereby "encounter" becomes perception of the actual situation, a way of reading off (not sizing up) what we are up against in it. The right identification of the powers moving in the actual situation, and the determination of the right response to and appropriation of those powers, cannot and is not in fact left in the hands of Intuition at all. For these transactions, therefore, some other account must be given. I shall try now to give a sketch of that account.

V

For this purpose let us begin with a primitive distinction between *recognition* and a kind of interpretation I propose to call *claiming*.

Recognition. In recognizing you I put you where you belong. On the basis of past experience I know what to make of you. The signals you have emitted heretofore, the symbolic structures ("language") you have characteristically employed for self-expression, fall into an intelligible and reasonably coherent pattern; so that even if you are at the moment erratic and inconsistent, I know exactly what I mean by *saying* that you are behaving erratically. If I do not know exactly what I mean by that, I have not in fact recognized *you*. Indeed, if you behave erratically enough I may cart you off to a doctor, on the interesting grounds that *you* are not *yourself!* That, let us note, is not a metaphysical judgment. It is a moral judgment. It means that your current behavior seriously jeopardizes your own best interests.

Claiming. In the example just given, I obviously claim a right (and perhaps even a duty) to act in your behalf; and I claim to know what your best interests are. Both claims are debatable. There are many occasions when they are not in fact debated because any reasonable person can see how the debate would come out, e.g., I am your father and you are a six-year-old boy. But even there the claim is debatable *in principle*. I cannot enforce my claims if I have been convicted of criminal negligence against you. In that case, even if I did actually know what would serve your best interests, I might be disqualified to serve as an agent for their protection.

There are other instances and kinds of claiming that are nearer the mark for our present theological interests and hopes. Consider this one. I make a claim upon your attention for the purpose of making a claim upon your loyalty and love. I suggest that this sequence is of some importance for the next stage of our argument.

"Listen to me! to *me*, the real being you are inclined to mistake or misread. I have a primordial right to be recognized as I *am* rather than as the (illusory) object of your desires and hopes and fears."

Now this does not obviously mean that the I is *worthy* of attention because of some achievement. The primordial right to be recognized is itself a function of a particular situation. *The claim upon attention, in other words, is the way a given structure operates.* I have in mind the parent-child relationship. The father ought to listen to the son, whether or not the son is "good"; and this takes precedence, oddly enough, over the obligation of the son to listen to the father. The reason for this is simple and compelling. The son depends upon the attention of the father in a way quite different from the way the father depends upon the son, and this is true quite independently of the encompassing social system.

The claim upon attention ("listen to *me*") is generally made with a view to making a claim upon love and loyalty. This does not automatically mean that the claimant supposes that one thing and one thing only will satisfy the claim. The claimant *may* mean that whatever is done, on the strength of an authentic and veracious recognition, must be done lovingly, even if what ensues is a flat denial of the material claim. We all know, of course, how badly mixed up this business gets in everyday human transaction: "If you really love me you will give me a new car," for example. This is but to say that claims upon love are often exploitive. This, however, has nothing to do with the logic of claiming. Again, that logic is simple: A serious and clear claim upon love and loyalty presupposes a claim upon attention, and the claim upon attention presupposes a capacity for recognition.

Now how much of this logic is available for the illumination and ordering of our business with God? The sketch I am proposing has several components.

1. Consider first the ancient prophetic formula, "The word of the Lord came to me and said. . . . " What follows (as in the case of Amos) is apparently a direct claim of the selfsame Lord upon the loyalty of his people. It is a demand for obedience to the law of the Covenant. It is far from clear, in any of the Old Testament prophets, that the prophetic spokesman for God rests his case upon some extraordinary experience of his own, or that he says God is the object of a direct intuition. The people of the Covenant *are* called to remembrance—to a recognition, if you please: They are the Lord's, and he has always provided; to them he has "revealed his arm." Thus they are summoned to a recognition of God's claim upon them.

2. Whatever we make of the theology of the prophet, and specifically whether or not we believe the prophet, has something uniquely informative to tell us about *God* himself, we can make out what sort of human claim is being made by the prophet. The whole history of the people

and, beyond that, all of life and the world are claimed for God. This means that the life of faith consists in part of viewing and construing the whole works as belonging to God. Especially the vital center of personal life, the "heart," is claimed for the tabernacle of the Lord, "the house" or tent of flesh-and-spirit.

The affective-volitional depth of the claim thus registered ought in itself be an adequate warning against any philosophical effort to interpret the prophetic claiming as anything like the posting of a hypothesis or a conjecture to be tested by experience and accepted if sufficiently confirmed. The force of the claim and the centers of life upon which it is trained so far leave nothing to tentativeness or to mental reservation. We are deeply attached to the spirit of tentativeness, of testing in order to see whether the Lord is there at all and not merely whether he is good; but we ought not to begin to explain this in terms of philosophical prepossessions, e.g., an antecedent and binding commitment to open-grid intelligence, revisability of all truths, relativity of all values, etc. I suggest that the beginning of an explanation is much more practical and historical; our century has seen what awful destruction fanaticism can wreak once it occupies the seats of power, and this whether the fanatic is revolutionary or counterrevolutionary. Beyond this is the overwhelming success of science, both in its theoretical probing of nature and its technological reconstruction of our lives. And since science in our understanding is committed to the revisability of all its beliefs and results, we have a model of the open-grid intelligence which honors no absolutes save Intelligence itself.

But what would naturally and clearly lead one to suppose that religious belief and commitment are but an extension into the depths of feeling and appetition of human curiosity and desire to control so much of human life and the environment as possible? In the religious life we are at once struck by the preeminence of the belief that here at last the "sense for the whole" is gratified; or, if it is not, one can discover where the deficiency is. I do not mean to suggest that the religious life is one with the conviction that "life is worth living" or with "my life is worth living." The sentiments are too vague; and they are too lightly attached to the decisive centers of human action, at least as they are commonly expressed and received. Rather, the religious life expresses the sense of being able to endure all things and to hope for the best because the power and goodness which sustain the world are here at hand to sustain me. This sense, this conviction, and finally this commitment do not admit tentativeness into their final composition. Each of us has days of doubt about his beliefs. In each of us the "sense of the whole" unpredictably falters. None of us is spared the experience of proving irresolute and even treacherous in our decisive commitments. But we are sustained, and not merely endured or put up with. This is the belief that God puts a value on our existence that we cannot cancel, even at our worst, individually and corporately.

I have spoken of this as a belief. It is actually a "construing belief." A construing belief is rather more a *believing* than it is the finished product commonly suggested by *belief*. Thus a construing belief is an interpretation of some aspect of experience. But it may also be a program, a mandate, as it were, for interpreting all of experience and the world. Such I take *believing in God* to be.

3. The prophet (early and late) is a great one for saying for the Lord God: "If you believe in me you will do thus-and-so." The formula quite naturally leads us to think that the doings constitute a series of inferences drawn off a budget of linguistic units called "beliefs," e.g., "God is love" *implies* "Love your neighbor." Now in fact "God is love" does not imply "Love your neighbor" in any easily recognizable sense of implication. Why not? Well, to start with, God is God and I am I; and unless one has already adopted a theology that cannot or will not distinguish God from me, I should have to say that what God is *able* to do entails of itself nothing whatever as to what I am *supposed* to do. Christians believe that God loves the whole works, with the possible exception of the Devil and the damned; but even of them we must say that if God does not love them they have no raison d'être, and therefore in the sight of God they are nothing. Not, note, *worse* than nothing; because in the traditional ontological scheme whatever totally fails to be cannot be the subject of a moral judgment, human or divine.

Furthermore, "God is love" might be taken to mean that God does not have to put the slightest effort into loving; he *is* love, by nature or essence. On the other hand, "Love your neighbor" stands over me as a prescription, as an imperative. "No commandment give I unto you except that you love one another as I have loved you." The prescription is notoriously hard to enforce, whether one thinks of it as commanding a feeling or passion or as laying down a policy norm. I do not mean that failure to obey the commandment is something the Christian is inclined to take lightly. He may, indeed, agonize over the failure and believe that his repeated failure rightly to love others (particularly his enemies?) is observed with severe displeasure in heaven and that sooner or later the divine displeasure will cut him off from "the land of the living." These dark forebodings and harsh self-accusations are not promising ground for the seeds of love. So Christians are constantly tempted either to vaporize the love commandment or to evacuate it. It is vaporized when "love" becomes a vague amiability and a readiness to wish well for almost all God's creatures. The love commandment is evacuated when one decides that at least one can try to "do right" by as many of the victims of injustice as one can manage without disrupting one's own life or upsetting the applecart of established society, and all the while resenting the bloody mess which other people have made of the world.

For the little it may be worth, we might note that we are up against a kind of logical puzzle here, as well. How can a statement about a state of affairs *imply* a prescription for action? Take a humdrum example. Some one has made a mess of my garden. Who ought to do something about it? You say, "The culprit, if you can catch him." You will probably not say, "Whoever or whatever is to blame, the same must make amends, tidy it up, etc." For it might have been the prankish wind, upsetting the trash cans and spreading the contents fortuitously to create the most offensive result. I can hold the wind responsible, in a manner of speaking, but I cannot put the wind under an imperative. It blows where it wills. I might pray that tomorrow it would blow from the opposite direction, but the effect of that might be to strew my neighbors' gardens with the same junk. If they knew I had prayed for that it might be a strain on community relations.

So only if the state of affairs is such that human agents are sensibly and enforceably chargeable with its ills can a statement to that effect be said to imply a prescription binding upon specific human agents. But that means that the very statement about the state of affairs already makes a claim upon ethical conviction and is intended to function as a moral constraint and motive. "God is love; thereafter, love your neighbors" does not look at all like that.

Perhaps, then, we are satisfied that the connection between the fundamental beliefs of the Christian and certain actions and patterns of action is not strict implication. Then what is it? It is a kind of inference. It is, actually, a whole bunch of inferences, as I shall now try to show.

4. Belief in God is a construing belief. It is in fact the supreme construing belief, but only in part because God is believed to be the Supreme Being. It is the supreme construing belief because it commands the widest range of routes of inference from antecedent factors to consequences, some of which function as confirmations of antecedent factors. Take, for example, the belief that God is Creator of all things

and Lord over all. (Even at the analytical level we ought not to construe "Creator of all things" and "Lord over all" as synonymous. For God might have started the show and left it thereafter pretty much if not altogether to its own devices and fate. Secondly, the Lord over all might not have started the show but might have demonstrated his competence and power to run it out to the end, whether or not he has any power or authority to change the end or postpone or hurry it, etc.) This belief is a declaration of intention both to "see" all things as belonging to God and actually so to construe them. Here "construe" is more than a linguistic-intellectual activity. *It means an intention to relate to all things in ways appropriate to their belonging to God.*

(I think it is important to enter a caveat here. This does not mean some kind of generalized application of the I-Thou principle to cover natural entities as well as persons; because the I-Thou, in my view, does not apply monolithically and univocally even to persons. Given forms of society not organized as *communities* [in the prevailing sociological understanding of community], I can and I must relate to those structures in ways appropriate to their nature [their being what they are]. Practically this means that it is not morally wrong *sometimes* to treat human beings impersonally, so far as I do not intentionally treat them as less than human. Impersonal treatment is not in itself brutalizing or cruel. Quite to the contrary, it is one of the prescriptions of *justice* that I should be able to abstract a moral concern from personal investment and private interest, in order to assure that persons and groups of persons should get what they deserve. This means that on some occasions I must be ready to act in adverse interest, relative to myself, not because there is someone out there who counts for more than I do, in some absolute scale, but because the pursuit of some interest of mine [and of my dearest group, often enough] has deprived some other being of something more fundamental in the pursuit of a human existence than that particular interest of mine. Thus, it is right that I should surrender some of my property, according to a certain [definite] rule, if my continued possession of it diminishes access of another person to sufficient food, clothing, medicine, work, etc., to maintain or establish him as a viable member of the state. For this purpose it does not matter that I know him personally and am therefore disposed to treat him better—or worse—than the mass of unknowns who have a right to be treated as "sons and daughters of God.")

Thus the vitally important business of determining the appropriate response to God's creatures can be identified as a process of running out inferences, not from some axioms in the mind but from the "dispositions of the heart." Inference as such is a matter of "getting from one thing to another," where the antecedent is something firmly grasped (or, in the case of intellect, clearly known), and the consequent (the being toward which inference runs its appointed course) is something to be made out and thereafter gathered into the antecedent. The process thus expands and enriches the antecedent. (This fact makes difficulties for the axiom model.)

The running out or tracking down of inference, therefore, in the prime instance of belief in God, ideally issues in the recognition of someone or something. I do not know what to make of the other until I know who he is, but I cannot know who or what the other is unless I am predisposed to let him be himself; that is, enter the structure of communication carrying his full weight of value. If I am so predisposed (this invaluable *pre*disposition is what we ought to mean by "infused grace producing faith"), I can confidently expect the structure of communication itself to be modified by the appearance in it of the other with his full weight and profile of value. His authentic self-expression, in other words, may (quite literally) scare the hell out of me. The antecedent disposition to affirm his being may be badly rattled by his emergence as he really is. This is a formidable possibility, rather more formidable than the possibility of my discovering personal hostility. *His hostility may be trained upon the structure of communication, because he has learned that this structure characteristically deprives him of some of his value.*

We say, therefore, that the routes of inference must be kept open to radical criticism and sweeping revision. This necessity goes beyond any effort to cope with philosophical challenges to the structure of belief, for what is being challenged in our time and in ourselves is the good faith of the Christian and only incidentally the structure of belief. It is our readiness to track down or follow out the proper inferences of our professed goodwill and overflowing love for all of God's children that is being most effectively challenged.

The openness thus laid upon Christian faith and conscience is a claim made by God the Holy Spirit. That, of course, is a theological proposition, an appropriation of an element in the structure of Christian belief. It is intended also to provide yet another illustration of the claiming character of Christian faith. To believe in God is to claim the whole world for him; and it is also to claim for him the very ground on which we stand to profess our faith; and it is also to claim for him the sovereign right to command the entire range of our powers of recognition and response.

Why then do the Christian prophets of social revolution in our day make so little of the Holy Spirit as a vital link in the structure of Christian life and belief? Perhaps they feel that the traditional structures are obsolete, except for an item or two that can be salvaged as sanction for the revolutionary cause. This conjecture is borne out to a degree by the readiness of the contemporary prophets to claim the "historical Jesus" for the Cause, and Old Testament representations of the God of absolute justice. But how can someone living now have an "existential encounter" with the historical Jesus, unless the prophet is prepared to draw upon fairly abstruse doctrine of the contemporaneity of Christ, à la Kierkegaard? I am sure we can see how a Christian might want to claim Jesus Christ as his ethical model as he wrestles with the harrowing problems of conscience and contemporary society. But this seems very far from the existential encounter with Christ himself. So also for any existential encounter with the Lord God of Old Testament righteousness. Perhaps Moses had such an experience. Judaism has never appealed to the *experience* of Moses as a warrant for the Religion of the Law. Nor has it sought to perfect ways by which the faithful Jew could have some of Moses' experience.

On the other hand, belief in God the Holy Spirit has certain fairly obvious advantages for the work of the prophet. Here is a representation of God, fully and truly God, everlastingly committed to making the kingdom of God intimate and precious to all men everywhere, through the ministry of the church and through other channels known only to God; and all this in a way absolutely faithful to the power and form of life manifested in the life, suffering, death, and resurrection of Jesus Christ. Here, furthermore, is a recognition of God governing history in his own way, imposing his own "logic" upon the flow of events in the world here below: not thinking as men think, not judging as men judge, ignoring human canons of justice and injustice, having no regard for towering human achievements, refusing to be impressed by worldly pomp and circumstance, granting eternal happiness to some anonymous character who offers a cup of cool water to someone in need and withholds it, apparently, from a high-minded citizen who has observed every detail of the Law. Surely here is a religious model of God moving with absolute freedom through the labyrinths created by Man to conceal himself from the piercing invincible demands of divine righteousness. Finally, in God the Holy Spirit faith has a model of God the Interpreter. It is he who brings *recognition*, of himself first and thereupon of ourselves, each bound to the other and to all others in a community of God's creation. Therefore the life of faith, that complex, formidable and withal exhilarating affair of construing all things as belonging wholly to God, opens before us, beneath us, over us, around us.

The Christian prophet, accordingly, would have excellent grounds for insisting upon an encounter with God as his justification and inspiration. This would be God the Holy Spirit, the sanctifying Presence before, so to speak, the eschatological Presence. Here encounter is as existential as you please. For this God is not *out there* as an empirically identifiable entity or power among other empirically identifiable entities and powers. But neither is he *in here* as a feature or quality of the hidden psyche or of the private soul struggling desperately or dreamily to maintain purity against the wickedness of the world out there. Rather God the Holy Spirit, the sustaining and sanctifying Presence, is apprehended as the mediating power rendering Being acceptable to beings, if you want a dash of ontological language. Or, in the language arbitrarily chosen for this occasion, mediating the antecedent disposition of faith to the potential consequences, potential not in the abstract scheme of Being and nonbeing but in the context of moral decision. The ethical other, that is, exists in his full profile and weight of value. But what he and I *may become* together, in conflict and in harmony, is yet to be made out. Somewhat fantastically I have used the term *inference* for that concrete process by which such potentialities are tracked down. The process or act by which they are realized is, of course, *decision*; and thereafter it is the giving and receiving of promise or pledge.

But perhaps the very openness demanded by encounter with God the Holy Spirit tends to minimize the acceptability or appropriateness of God so represented for the purpose of the contemporary prophet. Perhaps he needs to feel absolutely sure of his grounds. Perhaps he needs an *ultimate* justification for his posture and policies. Perhaps he is predisposed to believe that there is only one right course to be taken and endorsed through the thicket of modern life.

Pursuit of such considerations would precipitate us either into ad hominem arguments or into psychological exploration. The prophets themselves show some familiarity with both moves. I do not believe that this imparts either dignity or fertility to them—either to the moves or to the persons making them.

VII

Prophetic or otherwise, the Christian is still left with a very old and very pressing question. How does he distinguish the presence and work of God from the other powers in and of the world, making for its improvement? Among the prophets there were, of old, "lying spirits." The faithful community had therefore to discover some way to discern the true prophet and thereafter to dispose of the false ones. A similar problem arose very early in the Christian community. I believe it persists into our own life. How ought we to cope with it? I have no novelties to propose and must therefore fall back upon the tradition, as follows.

1. Whoever claims to have learned something directly from God for the reproof of the faithful community and for the building up of the human commonwealth must show that he speaks and lives from the "antecedent disposition." If, that is, he does not "speak the truth in love," he does not speak *God's* word at all. This does not rule out any chance of his saying important and productive things. It rules out an effective appeal to the "God and Father of our Lord Jesus Christ" as the decisive justification for his performance.

2. If the "word of the Lord" has indeed come to him personally, the claims he makes upon powers of recognition and enactment will have an element of novelty. They will be shocking, almost certainly. But the novelty will be a route of inference running from where the faithful now stand (or sit) to where they ought to be. The true prophet, in other words, is not so much concerned with disclosing new objects for acceptance and action as he is in showing that a reorientation of the antecedent disposition is now called for *by God*. No one is surprised when Jesus says, with the Law and the Prophets, "Love your neighbor as yourself." The surprise comes in the disclosure of the neighbor's identity; he is *anyone* in need of your attention and help. In terms of the particularities of our own situation as Christians in America, we do not need prophets of the Lord to tell us that the black community has an enforceable claim upon our sense of justice. *The double-edged sword of prophetic truth must fall upon the factor of exclusivism in the antecedent disposition of the faithful.* Thus Racism is not the primordial sin of American life. The primordial sin is the division in the antecedent disposition. We all believe that the love of God in Christ Jesus is compatible with attachment to preferential arrangements of many sorts in which Ego and Ego-like are automatically Master. Thus even the Black (and the Red and the Yellow) is let into the preferential community if he can show that he is *really* like us.

3. The true prophet of the Lord is therefore the declared enemy of anything and everything that divides the human commonwealth into warring factions. The true prophet is not a breeder of suspicions, hostilities, and alienations. He is an enemy of false harmonizations. It does not follow that he is the friend of disruption.

4. Both the prophet and the faithful community must therefore work from and with a normative model of the human commonwealth. The working models are inadequate, and they may be corrupt. What then shall we do, to be saved? Shall we encourage the prophet to turn vision-ary·and produce a new model? The visionary is apt to consult Ideality first, as though that wondrous realm of being offered compositional models rather than clues, directives, solicitations, lures, etc.—offered, that is, unitary programs of what-to-do and how-to-do-it. That is an ontological mistake. We would not worry about it if it had not had momentous practical consequences.

There is an alternative to the imaginative freehand construction of a normative model of the human commonwealth. That is the kingdom of Christ presented, re-presented, and accepted as the ambience of the antecedent disposition of the Christian. So understood, the kingdom of Christ is not a blueprint for the rebuilding of the human common-wealth. Rather, it *is* the human commonwealth, as it is recognized and claimed by Almighty God, the Father of our Lord Jesus Christ.

To this we must add a dash of historical realism. The higher righteous-ness opened to the antecedent disposition as the guidelines for the inference-tracking of the Christian life does not promise Utopia as the logical and historical reward. It offers instead something inexhaustibly rich: Wherever a person accepts his identity as a member of the king-dom of Christ, he will surely come to recognize a brother or sister in every human being. Common beneficiaries of the righteousness of God, they can together construe the whole world as the object of God's antecedent disposition. To value the world after the model of God's valuing of it is the ultimate, as it is the fundamental, encounter with God in the conditions of this life.

In the world to come we shall know fully, even as now we are fully known. That is one version of the Christian hope. It is for me the most precious, as it is also the most terrifying, because the knowledge of which it speaks is at once so familiar and so wonderful. I mean that knowledge which is the perfection of love.

5

Secularity and the Transcendence of God

I

The aim of this chapter is to render a constructive account of Christian belief in God Transcendent. The use of the word theological is intended to distinguish this venture both from sociological inquiry and from philosophical speculation. I do not understand the distinction to be absolute, however. The Christian and the church need a firm foundation on which to construe the cultural situation, and today this means some kind of response to secularity. Hence the treatment accorded here to secularity is likely to bear some resemblance to sociological generalization. Moreover, Christian belief in God Transcendent is a case of metaphysical belief, and so the speculative philosopher may keep a jealous eye on any invasion of his territory. But the cultural situation is not the property of sociology, and metaphysicians do not have a divine appointment to police beliefs about reality. Accordingly, so long as a theologian does not presume to instruct either sociologists or philosophers in their respective trades, he does not need to feel obliged to accept either as tutor in his own.

I propose, therefore, first to lay out some features of a Christian belief in God Transcendent. The second objective is to provide an account of secularity that concentrates on the religious features of this cultural situation. But this second objective is as theological as the first, for it is pursued with an eye on showing that the sense a Christian can discover in secularity is superior to the account a secularist provides of the same phenomenon.

This chapter is reprinted from *Secularization and the Protestant Prospect*, edited by James F. Childress and David Harned. Copyright © MCMLXX, The Westminster Press. Used by permission.

II

Some sensationally easy victories over belief in God Transcendent have been scored by taking that belief at its picturesque worst. For example, Christians are represented as believing in a God who lives outside the world in a place called Heaven from which he sends out mysterious messages, and into which place he will someday collect the souls of the people of whom he approves. It requires neither sociological nor theological genius to show that this picturesque nonsense can make no intelligible or productive contact with the spirit of secularity. But what is thus represented as the Christian view has an antecedent defect as well: It is a gross distortion of Christian belief in God Transcendent. That judgment must seem a flat and presumptuous assertion, presumptuous because it clearly hints that there is something Christians ought to believe, whether or not they do. That there is such a rule of faith ought to be shown rather than merely asserted.

One way of showing it is to track down a meaning of transcendence that comports with the images of God in the New Testament, images that command and direct the attention of the Christian. This is the hazardous route I choose to follow here.

The principal image of God in the New Testament is a being of unchallengeable majesty and righteousness who binds himself to something he has created, thus securing the fulfillment of its essential possibility. It is therefore appropriate that this God should in good faith be called Father, Lord, Shepherd, since each such title in its own way calls attention to his self-binding pledge.

When thereafter it is said of God that he "dwells in unapproachable light [1 Tim. 6:16]" and in him "there is no variation or shadow due to change [James 1:17]," the Christian ought not to take such cryptic utterances to be dogmatic definitions of divine transcendence. In that direction lie religious and philosophical notions incompatible with the principal image of God in the New Testament. But what are the other possibilities?

1. God transcends the world in that he, rather than the world, has what is needed for the fulfillment of the world.

This notion is sometimes expressed in a formula of doubtful value: The world needs (depends upon) God, but God does not need the world. (World − God = 0. God − World = God.) This proposition suggests strongly that contemplation of a cosmic situation essentially different from the actual one would disclose an essential property of God's being, his aseity. So far as I can determine, the sole virtue of this speculation is that it might reinforce a religious intuition, i.e., that God is God no matter what happens in any actual or imaginable state of the universe. But it might also be construed as support for the notion that God could part with the world without the slightest sense of loss.

2. God's goodness (or, in more general terms, his value) surpasses the goodness of creation, in whole or in part; and this because there is no limit by which the goodness of God must be defined.

The heart of this notion is sometimes expressed thus: God has in himself all the value realized in diffusion through the universe. But many zigs and zags are required to make the substitute formula plausible, and in the process the essential image may be lost. For shall we say that God has in himself the perfection of the blooming rose, in any sense other than his knowledge of that phenomenon and his good pleasure in it? It is truly unfortunate that divine transcendence should be conceived as requiring God to say to any creature, "Anything you can do I can do better!" We ought rather to represent God's good pleasure in the blooming rose as the best reason in the world for its being there.

3. God transcends the world in that his wisdom in deploying his resources is unsurpassable—indeed, unapproachable—by any other being.

This notion is calculated to remind one that Christian belief in God Transcendent must resist powerful and subtle temptations to represent God as overwhelmingly powerful—able to do anything that occurs to him as being an opportunity to display his might—and thereafter as a being to be trusted and loved because of his unmatchable goodness. Perhaps there is comfort to be pressed out of the dialectical twin of this metaphysical-religious temptation: God in his righteousness is lovely beyond all mortal bearing and just happens to have power sufficient for his impeccable purposes. The third option has thus something of a mediating function, largely because it is the very essence of wisdom to mediate rightness of principle and loftiness of purpose to the solid factuality of the world. A wise person is one who can correctly estimate what is the case and render efficaciously thereto his apprehension of and commitment to goodness. By definition, God's knowledge of what is the case is faultless. Theologians concerned to maintain belief in God Transcendent must thereafter accept the task of showing how belief in his wisdom (that is, his unsurpassable mastery of the instruments appropriate for the realization of the loftiest ends) can be defended against the ever-mounting pressure of secularity.

This is what I shall now undertake. For the decisive New Testament

LEWIS AND CLARK COLLEGE LIBRARY
PORTLAND, OREGON 97219

image of God is that of a being of unapproachable righteousness and majesty of power who has thrown in his lot with the strangest of all his creations, man. And one of the oddest of all the achievements of secularity is a powerful, though hardly constant, conviction that such a gamble is anything but wise, whether made by men or gods.

III

What then is this cultural situation identified as secularity? The following components merit theological attention.

1. Loss of confidence in traditional religious systems. We can safely leave to sociologists to determine whether people in this society are becoming less religious. In the meantime I think we can be sure that many no longer entrust to any traditional religious system any significant fraction of their economic, social, and political power. Again, this is not to say that the generality of people have lost their religious beliefs. In some intellectualistic circles, to have thrown off the dead weight of such beliefs is an indispensable criterion of spiritual maturity. This seems not to be true of society generally, though it may also be true of motorcycle gangs.

2. Widespread confidence in the powers of science to solve the most urgent problems, both cognitive and practical, now confronting Western man if not mankind generally. This component of secularity is the natural brother of the first one. The loss of confidence in traditional religious systems is not a clear philosophical victory over religious outlooks. Rather, it is a matter of one erstwhile powerful social system being replaced by another one, and these events are rarely if ever largely or clearly rational exchanges. Traditional religious systems have been found to be less and less effective in administering human power; and this, again, is because something else now seems clearly to be better for this purpose. The general public may be momentarily interested in a crashing triumph of research science if it is made minimally intelligible. "Science has solved the Riddle of Life!" "Science has created life in a test tube!" "Science has discovered the cause of cancer!" Headlines such as these create sufficient interest in the general reader to induce him to read perhaps a third of the appropriate article, or at least look carefully at the revealing pictures and diagrams. But, "Astronauts land on the moon!" "Science can now let you choose the sex of your next baby!" "At last, a cure for cancer! (or for air pollution, sterility, impotency, poverty, etc.)"—*that* is the stuff of secularity, the cash-out of the scientific business in terms of prolongation of human life, the extension

of the boundaries of human power, rendering man comfortable, safe, and free from servitude to demeaning tasks.

Thus, to the degree that traditional religious systems reinforced, if they did not exalt, the sense of human life as transitory, weak, and vulnerable, and sought therefore and thereby to keep it in bondage to a presumptively divine order—to that degree, at least, such systems have been discredited by the growth of science. The educated person now is amply armed against ancient definitions of man's limitations and of his nature and destiny overall. The person of properly educated sensibility may still believe part of that religious picture, but provisionally, for some scientific discovery may shortly knock out that residue too.

Accordingly, secularity denotes a very heavy dependence upon science for significant revisions of outlook and policy, rather than upon philosophy or religion; for neither philosophy nor religion has played an important or perhaps even a measurable role in the reshaping of the daily world. The scientist is the architect of this world. The contractor is the engineer. And the private creed of either or both is of no consequence as a factor in the prosecution of the social functions to which they are ordained.

3. Preoccupation with the daily world. We err when we construe this as a philosophic triumph of time over eternity, of nature over supernature. Those heroic conflicts matter very little to the daily world. Whether it is made in an antic or in a solemn spirit, an announcement of the death of God may at the discretion of the editor be placed under either the religion or the obituary column. It would be read by more people if the latter, by the putatively more thoughtful if the former.

4. Preoccupation with effective instrumentalizing of unquestioned ends and taken-for-granted purposes. This is a prime feature of the daily world. In this we may begin to make out the dense and momentous connections of secularity with the daily world. I do not mean to suggest that long-standing views of man's proper end are still decisive in this age, for they are not. Rather, the point is, again, the role of science in the modern persuasion that the right order and volume of instruments are at last available for the perfection of human life. Indeed, the point can legitimately be made stronger: The right attack on instrumentalization itself leads to the proper revision of ends and purposes. So again the inveterate disposition of religious systems to stress the fixity and finality of the human good as such runs afoul of a fundamental disposition of secularity.

It does not follow from this and it is probably not true that people generally (the denizens of the daily world) have become desensitized to religious experience as such. They may in fact crave more vividness and pungency in the line of religious experience than the traditional religious systems are providing.

5. A quest for the holy beyond the precincts of the sacred. The traditional theological distinction, sacred/secular, does not throw much light on the daily world and the secular spirit. For that purpose much more needs to be made of the distinction, holy/profane.

To hold something as holy is to elevate it above random, coarse, and abusive treatment; the holy is whatever cannot be safely profaned. Sacrilege, on the other hand, is an assault upon the sacred; it can be either deliberate or accidental, conscious or unconscious. Profanation is a matter of policy; it aims at dirtying something seriously held to be pure. Such a policy does not presuppose that nothing is holy. It does presuppose that something reserved as sacred is not holy. So one might seriously believe that something really holy has in fact been profaned by a religious insistence that it is sacred, and thereafter one might devote great energy and skill to attacking that barrier in the hope that the holy might come into its own. If, that is, one believed that sexuality were holy, one might attack the sacred institutions that have effectively made it dirty and/or trite. And if one believed that freedom were holy, one might well feel inspired to attack the sacred institutions that have effectively corrupted it. Thus the sacred emerges as that which men have arbitrarily demarcated as exempt from judgment and change and thereafter have used to protect a stake demonstrably narrower than the common good of mankind.

Secularity liberates man from bondage to the sacred and thus permits and encourages him to find the holy where and as he pleases or must. It tends, therefore, to make religion diffuse and idiosyncratic. Free to range beyond the precincts of the sacred, where might one turn next to find and grasp the holy? Prophecy is in order, but not prediction.

6. A profound and powerful tension between the daily world and ecstasy. If the secular spirit has succeeded in generalizing the holy beyond the arbitrary limitations of the sacred, it has in that scored an ambiguous victory. For suppose that the pursuit of the holy is felt to be necessarily ecstatic. Who can tell how far beyond the boundaries of the daily world one may be carried by the power of the holy? Yet secularity operates effectively as such only upon the basis of images and concepts of a bounded and normal world, even though the boundaries are no longer fixed by divine fiat. Wherein then is its victory if, by fair

means or foul, souls aspiring for largeness and vividness of life break free of those putatively human limits?

We come thus upon a human phenomenon with which religious systems have been contending throughout history, and if the secularist learns nothing from this encounter let him blame no one but himself. This is the phenomenon of self-transcendence, the inextirpable human urge to break beyond the boundaries of self and self-reflecting world into a unity, power, and beauty unattainable in the daily world and thus inexpressible in its terms.

This human phenomenon prompts grave questions of a theological order, whatever the religious dispositions of the theologian. I propose now to state and consider some of those theological questions. They all have to do with a singular fact: namely, that man is obliged to put together powerful presentments of three worlds, and in a way that does not permit any of the three to block access to the others. But here, surely, is a great mystery: Each of the worlds presses upon the individual spirit the great benefits of routinization, but each hints of ecstasies to break past the routines of the others.

IV

The three worlds that lay unavoidable claims upon human life are:

The daily world (Q, for quotidian)
The world of nature (N)
The ideal world (I)

We have, therefore, two prime questions about man's relation to any or all of these worlds: (1) What mode of human transcendence is proper to each of them? (2) How ought the Christian construe God's transcendence in relation to each of the worlds? The proper pursuit of these questions requires initial clarity in the identification of the plural worlds. So this is the immediate task.

Q is the world that claims us in that set of standard beliefs, dispositions, attitudes, and overt gestures invoked by reference to what everybody knows, believes, hopes, and does. It is thus a commonsensical system: Its values are prima facie; its truths are taken for granted. It is what claims us again when ecstasy is over. It is that state of affairs in which we do not need merely to guess at how work, play, and love will be appraised, for its rewards and punishments are not reserved for eschatological disclosure.

Q cannot help but put a high value on stability of social structure and individual character, and upon instrumental intelligence and prudential wisdom. The Q component in human life is dedicated to keeping the show on the road, keeping the store open, making do, getting by, hoping to recoup tomorrow today's losses. It is the world in which discretion is the better part of valor, but it knows how to reward valorous defense of itself.

N is the world upon whose routines Q tries to establish its own, for otherwise the human does not emerge in its own right at all. Thus, man must eat to live; that is a law of N. But in order to live he ought not to eat his brother; that is a law of Q. If a man is starving he may obey N rather than Q, but he might not, too; and thus in critical cases Q and N jostle each other a good deal. But Q is aware of the pressure from N, and N probably does not care.

Thus the genetic code is Nature's business. Man is learning very rapidly how to butt into that business on purpose; that is, both to learn how it works and to improve his situation, rather than blindly to change it and be changed by it. But beyond all such explorations, appropriations, and explanations there is an ongoing show in which man plays a very small role, and in which there is nothing or no one to remember him when his brief and uncertain day is done.

So Q and N intersect only so far as Q is disposed or required to do so for its own sustenance. Q is essentially teleological; if the orders and powers of the daily world fail to execute their particular purposes, they are modified and even abrogated. N is not so patently teleological. To know about N is a great human interest, fertilized by access to the ideal world (I). We do not know that N gives a fig for that itch. One can of course say that a cognitive appetite is the read-off of certain genes. I doubt that anything could be a clearer case of the pathetic fallacy than to ascribe to some genes a desire to learn about the rest.

The ideal world (I) overarches Q. The relations of I to N are essentially problematical. I includes both the possible and the desirable, the not-yet and the ought-to-be. There is a simple difference between these, so far as "X may very well happen" is plainly different from "I hope to God X never happens."

I overarches Q, and it may in some feature or other pervade Q as well. For Q is among other things a system of expectations, both great and small. England expects every man to do his duty through hell and high water. It is expected that you will pay your taxes. Thus the inevitabilities of Q: death and taxes. But one can renege on both, up to a point, and with warrants drawn on I. An individual can refuse to do his manifest duty and say a higher duty supports his refusal. So also for taxes. As for N, if he is properly shot for shirking his duty, he will die. This is nothing to N—from dust to dust—and the commotion in between is of no concern. But it matters greatly to Q. Fundamental challenge to its fundamental routines cannot be ignored.

Nonetheless, fundamental challenges of Q are inspired by access to I. The daily world is open to all kinds of criticisms that go beyond the working assumptions of Q and that may in fact put those assumptions under direct fire.

But N can also be reached by I through the mediation of man. Obedient to a vision of a good—or at least a better—society, men may decide to use natural resources in a way different from the routines of Q but yet compatible with some of Q. But does I make any difference to N when man is not around? Is N itself somehow obedient to I? Or is I by itself (that is, taken in abstraction) without life?

Such questions lure us out on the deeps of metaphysics and religion. We are not ready for that trip, though we are nudged toward the depths whensoever we properly consider the readiness of Q to justify itself in its relations to N and to itself by appealing to I—but also to justify itself to God.

Q's appeal to I in order to checkmate individual access to I (or, for that matter, to God) is a good point at which to ask the first of the theological questions mentioned above. This is one of the important ways in which Q is (and not simply employs) a system for routinizing human self-transcendence. The ecstatic breakaway from Q into I is a formidable possibility at every moment in the life of Q, for there is no telling when doubt about the finality of Q's routines will ascend into sublime certainty that Q is the shabbiest of lies rather than a systematic and fitfully benign illusion. There is nothing for it then but for Q to insist that everything in I pertinent to the ordering of human life is already available in Q. This can be brought off with a fair measure of philosophic subtlety, as follows.

Perhaps I is not a world at all but is the product of human imagination and need and is therefore to be grounded in Q. Surely men tend to imagine that the inadequacies of their Q could be relieved if all agreed now to do such-and-so. But there is precious little uniformity in what they thus imagine, partly because Q worlds suffer from a very wide range of inadequacies, and partly because men draw upon I for all sorts of remedies. Moreover, Q and I are really one world, for I is a set of idealizations of Q, and Q is a systematic response to the demands of I. So I supplies cues and directives for the ordering of Q, given the actualities of N.

It would seem to follow that I is nothing in itself, or is at best the invention of philosophers who are not quite able to cope with Q.

This sort of effort to corral human self-transcending in the direction of I is now in woeful disrepair. Given the very wide diffusion of Freudian and Marxian theologies, this is a very curious situation indeed. One is tempted to believe that the very success of these secularizing theologies has driven the most sensitive spirits into the idealistic ecstasy. But surely there are other telling factors in the crisis of secularity. One of these is the merciless pressure of that dimension of I called the not-yet.

Here again Q puts on a brave face, for Q cannot endure unless its constituents believe that it is an effective time binder. Here is the only history that matters, and here is the route to the future. Or put it this way: Q cannot get away with its claims upon human energies and loyalties unless it advertises a successful administration of death as well as of life. This does not mean that death is the prime case of the not-yet. It does mean that every routinization of expectation in and as Q is already an awkward acknowledgment of death, death for the individual and for this Q and for all Qs. Thus the Q in which we live cannot yet make up its mind about the legal taking of life. Death still lingers as an instrument of policy, but the traditional theological-ethical appeals to the common good of mankind as a justification for such an instrument are now more than faintly tinged with desperation and with other elements of bad faith.

The idealistic ecstasy is not the only way out of Q. Even now it shares the stage with the naturalistic ecstasy. This requires some device for releasing biological vitalities, a device that momentarily suppresses individuality and personality and lets life flow in primordial unity and potency. Here the end in view is, paradoxically perhaps, to overcome the teleological system of society-and-self and escape at once the niggling erosions of Q and the relentless pressure of the not-yet.

So where the idealistic ecstasy counsels, "Become what you ought!" the naturalistic ecstasy counsels, "Throw off the criminal restraints of Q and I and simply enjoy!"

How then is the loyal inhabitant of Q, antecedently convinced that Q is enough for his life, to thread his way among the options in a time when nothing about Q is more uncertain than its capability for making a coherent routine out of the thrust for self-transcendence? The problem goes from strength to strength, and the tranquillity of Q is shattered into the predictable future.

Yet the very existence of Q is an achievement of human transcendence vis-à-vis N, the world of nature. Powerful philosophical minds in the modern world have sought to resituate man in the bosom of Nature, partly in reaction to the idealistic absorption of Nature into Spirit, and partly in positive response to the astonishing scientific triumphs of evolutionism. Nature thus celebrated is not the affair of ordinary experience. It is just as certainly not the value-free affair that emerges from scientific treatment of ordinary experience. The Nature of naturalist philosophical evocation lures man—construed as being far more plastic than classical metaphysics could allow—into creativity marvelously harmonious with the inarticulate powers of life elsewhere in the cosmos.

But, again, this is not the feel of the nature with which Q man must contend. Indeed, the Q world is at best an uneasy truce with N. Q is an achievement of human creativity, too. It is a system of make-do in the face of N. And even where the public face of N is bland and smiling all the day, there are still the formidable powers of the night, and death is not friendly.

Nevertheless man's access to I, the ideal world, does not let him take even the greatest triumphs of Q as final. If, for the sake of Q, N in us must be sublimated, Q itself must yield to the pressure of the ideal. For no Q is sufficiently humane. In every Q, precious things must be sold off to keep the days moving in steady, sensible procession. Thus Q inevitably comes to prize routine quite as much as N and has no greater success than momentarily convincing us that its routines are really a matter of "doing what comes naturally."

It would seem, then, that I is the transcending world itself and is not itself meaningfully or creatively transcended. What higher ecstasy could be portrayed than union with the ideal world, no longer to perceive it dimly and from a great distance, but at last to be in it as what one ought to be, *sub specie aeternitatis?*

The perennial attractiveness of this notion testifies to persistent ambiguities in the concept of transcendence, some of which we have already reviewed. The severest difficulty with the view is not, however, any of its ambiguities. Rather, it is its distrust of the actual, of which Q is but one formation and one object of suspicion. For the actual is a break in the chain of ideal necessity; it stinks of contingency, not only of "It might have been otherwise" but also of "Who knows how it will turn out?"

Thus, actuality has its own mode of transcendence vis-à-vis I. Whatever is actual has a solidity of being in principle denied I. This solidity of being is the joy of all desiring in Q. Q is trying to be actual, in other words. This is its peculiar glory and its peculiar wretchedness as well. But even in the depths of its misery it is better off than I, because I has no power in its own right at all. I can claim but it cannot enforce. Q can enforce, and it is always being tempted to identify this power as the essence of rightful claim, which it is not.

But we must not overlook the fact that the actual is an individual rather than a system or an order. This is the seat of Q's wretchedness, since Q is a system. System is something created by actual individuals as an extension and/or synthesis of their powers. Thus Q has about it a remarkable illusion: namely, that there is no meaningful life outside it, whereas in fact the actual individual is already outside it, so far as he is actual. As actual, he is already living into a future, a not-yet, about which Q can really do nothing better than to say, "Who knows what will happen?" Moreover, the actual individual is that, is actual, because he is already a synthesis of existence and possibility and of fact and value. The actual is a realization, the proper or essential fixity of which is a value rather than a fact. Fact is what has happened and, as such, is forever immutable. But the actual is an aim-being-realized, a good being materialized. Upon this process I impinges only through the envisagements of actual individuals. N is there to receive the results. Q is the systematic minimal assessment of their value.

V

God is the supremely actual, the quintessentially individual. The key to his transcendence of all the worlds is thus to be found in his actuality.

As a human creation, Q is a tragicomic analogy of N as God's creation. Man is an artificer. So are the beaver and the paper wasp. They build to protect themselves against nature: unfriendly elements and predators. Yet they are thoroughly situated in this same nature; they do not deny, hinder, or worship it. But man is the Q maker. He believes his creation partakes of divinity because it is a world, whereas beavers and wasps can boast only colonies.

Viewed theologically, there is no mystery about God's transcendence of any and all Q worlds. He is beyond any power to contain him that any or all Qs might boast. Indeed, he belongs to none of them; none is an object of particular divine concern. For if the human person as actual does not live either in or for a Q world, why should God?

As for N, it is God's creation. He is in it only so far as any artist is in his work. But this does not mean that N is best construed, theologically, as a flat, static, and thus uninteresting backdrop for some historical drama. Indeed not. Perhaps there is not life everywhere in the system of nature. But wherever there are actual individuals, there is assuredly life: energy under the control of appetition, and appetition responsive to the good.

Thus again the tragicomic character of the Q world, for N itself is not all routine. God has not left it indifferent to chance and novelty. And if there are bloody enmities in it, none is predicated on the assumption that N is not big enough for all the warring species. Furthermore, so far as N is a living system at all, it is symbiotic, a harmonium of ends rather than irresolvable conflict.

I, the ideal world, must seem at first glance somehow dearer to God's life than any other world. Or have the idealistic ecstatics and metaphysicians misled us on this matter? They have, I think. What God, himself supremely actual, is after is actuality; or, rather, actualizations. That is why Christians believe that man is created in God's image. But this does not mean that God seeks imitations—godlets, simulacra, repetitions. As actual, God is altogether disposed to the maximization of value. So far he may properly be said to depend upon ideality, even if it is a feature of his own being. In God, the tug of the ideal is the ultimate reconciliation of the ought-to-be and the might-be, the good and the possible. He is what the entire cosmic (and this includes the historical) process is struggling to become. In picture language, God is out there in the future. This does not mean that he has already experienced what has not yet happened on earth or elsewhere in the affairs of actual beings. It means that God's envisagement of the good binds the entire cosmic process toward its realization.

VI

How then is God Transcendent, the supremely actual individual, related to human actuality? Here we return to the primordial Christian image of God: that being who binds himself to his creation for the fulfillment of its possibility.

"Man" is a name, not primarily of an ideal, however splendid, but of an actuality, a living synthesis of existence and ideality.

Thus man functions in rightly ordered human life as an ideal. The word *man* names a commonwealth not yet visible and palpable, a state of affairs that includes everything human and in which everything included is affirmed.

So identified, man is an inordinately harsh judgment upon any and every Q world. Every Q legislates exclusions, some of which are relative and some absolute. In our Q, the poor are excluded from the promise and the instrumentalities of that self-improvement presumably at the heart of the American Dream. The black man is excluded from preferential living districts. It is a tender part of the American theology to believe that no one is absolutely excluded from some of the proper benefits of this society. Yet we license the killing of capital offenders against this society. That is a fair example of an absolute exclusion. Belief in a divine everlasting punishment is another one.

God intends the overcoming of all exclusivist structures and principles. That is why we say that no Q is an object of particular divine concern, except in the sense of God's unalterable opposition to anything that hinders the flow of human life outward and upward into the commonwealth of man.

Thus, God pledges his full support for every human aspiration to that commonwealth. But here God seems to be confronted with a choice: identifying with human individuals seeking to find themselves in love of others, or lifting human life bodily, so to speak, into his own life.

The proper novelty of the Christian view of God Transcendent is a settled determination to allow God to have it both ways. For the Christian believes that God is in Jesus Christ and Jesus Christ is God fully present to and with human beings. And the Christian believes that man is thus actualized as a member of the divine community. God is beginning and end, but in the end he is not by himself but has fellowship with man.

Human self-transcendence, therefore, in the Christian view is aimed at God. This is in no way a program or design for escaping from the world, if by "world" one means the human condition in space and time, fully exposed at once to the vicissitudes of life in N and the temptations of life in Q. Since the aim of man's self-transcendence is God, any significant achievement in that line is an acquisition of power to love the world as it ought to be loved; that is, passionately and wisely. Inevitably, therefore, the Christian life from its historical beginnings is construed as ministry to the world, looking toward the reconciliation of man to God and thus of men to man.

So it is the case that for the Christian the secondary aim of self-transcendence is the human commonwealth, man. We say "secondary" simply because in the Christian view one is not entitled to live for man unless first he lives to God, and not because man comes limping into the purview of the Christian only after he has said his prayers and put down his bets—hopefully in that sequence. But let us also be clear that this sense of the priorities, God first and then man, is not the product alone or perhaps even primarily. There is behind it some reflection upon human history, for in that tale man has often been loved and indeed served with ferocious ardor while actual human beings perished aforetime both for want of attention and from the unconscionable cruelty of fanatical visionaries. Thus both from history and the gospel the Christian may learn that man must descend from the I world, the realm of ideality, into the material circumstances of some Q world, in order to be perceived rightly and rightly loved. For love is richest and best when it goes out to and returns from an actual being, and there is no actual human being accessible to the normalities of intercourse who is not an inhabitant of some Q world.

But right here a momentous problem arises. If it is the case that the actual person lives beyond any and every Q by virtue of being actual, why is the typical encounter of person with person so deeply embedded in Q and bounded by Q's perimeters? For that is surely the feel of the matter. We seem therefore to be hounded all the way home by an astonishing paradox: It is in Q's best interests to make its people feel at home in it; yet, at least in our Q, "we are strangers when we meet." In fact our Q seems to be dedicated, insanely, to maximizing and generalizing alienation to its furthermost limits.

Again I must leave to the social scientist the task of tracing the kinds and magnitudes of alienation in this society. Here let me ask, rather, whether the rapid instrumentalizing of human life is not a prime cause of the paradoxical disquietude at the heart of Q. I believe this is the case. If it is the case, then any secularist gospel that celebrates some world as enough for any legitimate human aspiration had better be swift to identify what world that is. Surely the Q world is a very poor candidate for that election, if it is the case that the primacy of the use value of human life is our Q's contribution to the human commonwealth.

The truth about this Q may not be that bleak. We should hope that it is not, but we should not let hope blind us to the truth, whatever it is. In any case there is enough to be done to bring the standard levels of aspiration in this Q up to the requirements of actuality. It is not given to Q to redeem itself, but the actual agents living in it can certainly make it more responsive to the essential demands of man. This they can do only so far as they see God and resolutely obey him.

VII

Ecstatic breakaway from this Q of ours seems daily to become a strict necessity for more and more of Q's denizens. One of the accidental wonders of the technological society is the splendid proliferation of materials and techniques for ecstasy. Mankind has long possessed a variety of means for lowering consciousness to the vanishing point, and this immemorial lore of narcosis is remarkably similar to the practice of death. But now our Q seems quite as interested in consciousness-expanding ecstasy: the augmenting, rather than the diminishing, of human power. (This rather nicely exemplifies the profound ambiguity of freedom in this world—the flight from the arbitrary confinements of existence and the flight toward actuality.)

The traditional religious communities still extant in our Q world are predictably suspicious of all but the tamest ecstasies. This may be explained as so many expressions of a material concern for the well-being of Q. The concern and the suspicions may quite as well be misplaced and exaggerated, for the great mother of ecstasy is religion. Unhappily, our Q world may have become so preoccupied with religion as a powerful instrument of social control that religion as a disciplined ecstatic opening to God is concealed behind a dark cloud of suspicion. If this is the case, the Christian—church and individual—has a great and taxing work to do. For God in Jesus Christ draws all mankind into his own actuality. Therefore each human being is destined to be raptured out of the definition any normal synthesis of I and N and Q can achieve for him. And it will not do, for this divine purpose, to seek to postpone that ecstatic union with God until some final moment of the world-historical process. Upon whomever it dawns that this is the acceptable year of the Lord (and this as something incomparably richer and more powerful than an interesting item for belief), it will surely break in as ecstasy, as a pulling away from the roots and the boundaries of the normal world. When God, supremely and everlastingly actual, speaks as and for himself, what is really possible for man and therefore what is really desirable for us comes wonderfully into sight and sound and touch, and the normal world retires into its proper magnitude. It is, after all, something men have made. If it does not properly serve man, it cannot in any way glorify God.

VIII

There is very little empirical indication that the spirit of secularity is forging ahead without the benefits of religion, or at least of religiousness. To be sure, prophets of the new age, or of the great tomorrow, look forward with longing almost too great to be borne to the time when man can at last live in, for, and through himself. Since we are not there yet, and I think nowhere near it, the question remains whether there is religion that provides an opening toward God Transcendent, that being who cares infinitely about the fulfillment of man in actual persons.

Wherever Christians, individually and corporately, do not live in that faith, they are missing the point. Secularity at its best is an eloquent plea for the commonwealth of man. As such it is a powerful rebuke to Christians living in bad faith. But the proper response to such a rebuke is not to abandon the Christian faith. It would be better to practice it.

6

Modern Images of Man

This chapter is proposed as a fragment of the story generally identified as the conflict of the sacred and the secular in the modern world. It is the part of the story in which the imagination is the battleground; and the triumph of the secular is grasped as the ascendency of images of man in which his autonomy vis-à-vis any power and value greater than he is expressed.

Before we treat these images, we ought to be as clear as possible on the fundamental conflict of the secular and the sacred. I shall begin with several suggestions about this. Then a number of images in the conflict will pass in review. In an epilogue, a question is raised about the possibility of a reformation of the image of man.

Sociologists and other theologians largely agree that we are living in the Age of the Secular. Religious people who do not recognize this and adjust the forms of the religious life appropriately live under that awful threat, irrelevancy. Progressive religious thinkers, on the other hand, hail the secular spirit as a major advance into the kingdom of light. For the latter, secularism seems to signify the attainment of maturity for Western man after an unnaturally prolonged and complicated adolescence: Man has at last come of age; let us rejoice that he has put away childish fears and hopes. What, then, is this spiritual condition for and in which the sacred retreats before the irresistible advance of the secular? Here are some unsystematic suggestions.

1. It does not help very much to confuse *civil* and *secular* with each other; or *religious* and *sacred*. The civil state has taken over many public services once the preserve of religious communities, for example, care of the indigent and education of the young. These are hardly illustrations of the triumph of the secular. They are cases of things grown too

This chapter is reprinted from *The Central Conference of American Rabbis Journal,* June 1969, pp. 2-17. Used by permission.

massive for efficient and equitable management by any agent other than the state itself.

Moreover, it is possible to talk meaningfully about a civil religion, as Professor Robert N. Bellah has done in his famous essay, "Civil Religion in America" (*Daedalus*, Winter 1967). Some sense of the sacred is invoked in that religion, such as the covenant in which we are bound with all who have fought the good fight and kept faith with that God who demands of this nation that it make freedom, justice, and equality available for all who live in it.

In other ways the sense of the sacred slips away from the precincts of the religious forms which once governed it. One might think here of the "sacredness of human life," felt by many to be a more certain bulwark against the triumph of scientifically sophisticated brutality than the traditional forms of religion.

2. The tension between the sacred and the secular begins to come into its own when the sacred appears as the *inviolable* and the secular as the *manipulable*.

We begin by supposing that objects and places are the prime instances of the inviolable: the Holy of Holies, the Ark of the Covenant, the elements of the sacrament, etc. This is a foreshortened view of the matter. Places and objects are designated vehicles and condensations of sacred power; and they are designated by the sacred power itself, not by mere men. Accordingly what is sacred by divine designation—places, objects, persons—can be violated, de facto. A temple can be burned, befouled; in a word, *desecrated*. But if one believes that the temple is sacred by divine designation, one would say, I suppose, that it cannot be violated with impunity. Vengeance is mine, I will repay, says the Lord.

Are people greatly impressed by this threat of divine reprisal for sacrilege? That is a kind of social psychological question, and I am just enough of a theologian to be interested in it. So I judge that people are not so much impressed by this threat as their parents were. If that is the case, is it part of the triumph of the secular?

An unequivocal answer to that question would be difficult to defend. We would have to know several other things before we got on to that. For one, how has the inviolability of divine power been understood? With the metaphor of the river that spreads destruction all around when it is dammed? As an obligation enforced by profound guilt and anxiety when it is denied practical expression? As a punishment that gathers terror the longer its execution is postponed?

Other possibilities come to mind. One of them is remarkably close to a salient theme in contemporary philosophical religiousness: the silence of God. Out of the biblical past comes the word against those who have violated the inviolable: "Though you call upon me on that day, I will not answer, for your sins are multitudinous and you are unrepentant." Happily, this is still a long way from a classical Christian doctrine: namely, that God withdraws his sustaining grace from the wretched sinners in Eden, and they cannot therefore but be confirmed in sin and guilt until God himself in mysterious mercy lets his grace again abound. Even so, the prophetic threat is sufficiently terrible, because it means that though God takes notice of his people's plight he will not speak the saving word. From the immensity of the punishment we learn more about the enormity of the offense than its commission alone would have provided.

Now again the silence of God has become a philosophical religious theme. It is in Heidegger, notably. It appears in radical Protestant theologians who are considerably more instructed by the achievements of secularism than they are by the profundities of Heidegger. The note of inviolability of divine power is missing from both; the divine silence is not an expression of divine judgment. Yet Heidegger believes that modern man is wandering in a dense thicket, a creature in a fair way to lose his soul beneath the ever-mounting pile of thing acquisitions or in the ever-deepening cloud of anonymity emitted from mass culture.

Thus something inviolable in the order of being takes shape, whether or not we are licensed to call it divine. If, that is, we say that the conditions of authentic existence cannot be violated with impunity, we are at the least saying, Being will not let us have it both ways: I cannot will both to be myself and to be your instrument; if I am the master of my destiny, up to death, then I cannot blame my lot on you or upon society, fate, or any other god. Put it paradoxically, and say that the requirements of freedom are inviolable and the penalty for violating them is bondage: a poor bargain. To make it poor and inescapable, a divine enforcer would seem to be unnecessary. That latter discovery does not clearly or simply redound to the greater glory of the secular spirit.

That spirit begins to take on substance when the question, "Do we need to suppose that anything is absolute and therefore inviolable?" receives an automatic negative. Heraclitus said, "Flux is king." He believed also that there is an eternal rational order. That sentiment excludes him from the spirit of secularity. Against the background of historic religion and philosophy in the Western world, the secular spirit stands forth as the intent to lay hands on human life and make something suitable of it without fear or expectation of interference or assistance from beyond. So disposed, men learn quickly that Nature, too, is a malleable thing; Nature is soon sliding down the order of being into pure instrumentality for human aggrandizement. If, thereafter, man were induced to see himself as a being entirely immersed in Nature, what would prevent him from going down the chute into pure instrumentality? We can throw off the subjunctive and say that modern man is in that descent. The doctrine of the sacredness of human life floats out behind like a small and tattered parachute, insufficient for anything except to mark the place where he lands, in case anybody misses him.

3. The sacred is the ultimately mysterious. The secular is the essentially resolvable.

Mysterious does not mean obscure or unknowable. There is nothing necessarily obscure or knowledge-defeating about love. If love be not palpable, wherefore should we call it love? Yet love is a mystery in two fundamental senses: One, it resists assimilation or reduction to anything else, and this is the primordial wisdom in calling love itself divine; and two, love has its own "reasons." What question is more common and less manageable than "Why do you love me?" Love is a great begetter of Why's; but it is begotten by none.

So far as the secular is the comprehensive imperium of the modern world, it seeks to resolve all mystery into the operationally manageable. Thus life was for many epochs looked upon as mysterious in its source; now science is close to producing the real thing synthetically. Once the mystery of amino acids was resolved, the great door to the creation of living matter began to swing open. The vista thus disclosed contains a more comprehensive control of human life than even old-time gods would have imagined for themselves. Having it, they would not have risked sharing it with mere men.

Reverence, then, is an emotion of dubious import for the secular spirit. For reverence casts an aura of transcendental value around some aspect or form of being, and whatever is thus endowed cannot be modified or reduced but must be humbly acknowledged and its graces devoutly petitioned and patiently awaited. There may be things in the secular imperium that ought to be fairly respected, but all boundaries therein and thereof are provisional. They may hold us up today. Tomorrow, or on some tomorrow, those boundaries will be penetrated and incorporated by the imperium of scientific man.

Two illustrations of this mentality come to mind. One is the drive to bring outer space within human utility. The other is the systematic penetration and reduction of personal privacy. In both directions the notion of immovable boundaries is an offense to the secular spirit. The power is not yet available to spread human ordure throughout the cosmos. The age has made splendid progress in persuading more and more people that the love of privacy for any purpose—defecation, copulation, or celestial meditation—is a destructive residue of ancient religion and, thank God, can at last itself be destroyed by the technological wizardry of the mass media. Why save your genitals for private consumption when millions can be blessed by a fearless demonstration coast to coast?

There is something odd about this situation. The mass media, which make possible the generalization of social protest from one place to many with the speed of light, nearly, are an indispensable part of a manipulative and exploitative social system. The movement which makes the dedicated use of four-letter words the key to existential freedom presupposes a system that makes nothing of the free exercise of reason; from which it appears that the only way to make a case is to be one.

4. The sacred relates man to transcendent being and value. The secular impulse is to deny either the reality of a transcendent realm or its accessibility. If that realm cannot be reached, why should we worry about it? The rhetorical question is an answer. Epicurus put it thus: If the gods exist and are aware of us, they would wish us well. To which we can properly add: Thanks for nothing.

"Transcendent" does not necessarily argue "religious." There are religions of immanence, celebrations of the here-and-now indifferent to what might be yonder and later. And there are intuitions of transcendence, the sense of magnitudes looming above the earthly scene that command loyalty but make no promises.

Nonetheless, one religious community or another has been native ground for the sense of the transcendent until now. We should hardly doubt that there it has too often mingled with obscurantist suspicions of rapid and inclusive social change. This may partially account for secularistic attacks on every transcendental element in religion, and for a spirit of toleration for *religious* understood as devotion to the human ideal, as well.

From this one might too swiftly conclude that *secular* and *humanistic* are properly synonymous. In fact, the sense of the transcendent does not rule out even the most evangelical affirmation of the importance of being human; and so far as the secular spirit is committed to the manipulation of human life, its humaneness may legitimately be questioned. Furthermore, we have come too far down that road to feel profoundly reassured when told that the human engineering now possible will surely be applied to man for his improvement. How wonderful it would be if all the hideous torments heaped upon human life in this century were but nightmares, diabolical dreams, and soon we should wake and thankfully shake off that horrid sleep. It is salty comfort to realize that far worse can be done than has been done.

It is in this area that the principle issue between the sacred and the secular is joined. The question is whether there are limits, both cosmic and personal, beyond which man may not pass and live, neither the intruder nor his posterity if they build upon his sacrilege. Hard upon that comes the next question: Are those limits observed—held, that is, in full survey from the other side or above—and enforced by transcendent power? Or is it just that man, going too far too fast, is bound to run out of steam and collapse, not in some place ordained for his execution, thither lured by some cunning observant god, but, rather, accidentally beside the road in the desert?

Whatever one's religious disposition, such questions unleash anxiety. For that there is no help in returning to believe again in vengeful Deity. That is a misdirected sense of the transcendent. It bespeaks a God who enters the human picture only to punish. Before such a being we might have to grovel; but we could not worship him, we would not worship him so long as any vital sense of human worth remained.

So the contest is for the imagination of man and for his loyalty. It is for his imagination, because he must have a vivid perception of his being and of his value if he is to stand tall among the other creatures of dust and claim his inheritance. But the contest between sacred and secular is for his loyalty, too. If he has no interests other than his own to serve, the sense of the transcendent can only confuse him; and he has enough to do to determine what he owes of earth's store and the blood's to generations yet unborn. If, however, he grasps in the mind's eye conjunctions of his interests with those of beings all around and beyond, then he ought to act as befits a steward rather than an absolute owner; for what he does matters everywhere and forever.

So much for a general account of the conflict of the sacred and the secular. We have now to consider eruptions of this conflict in the realm of images. This we do convinced that as the image goes so goes the man.

I do not intend to argue here the merits of that philosophical anthropological assumption.

The Darling. One of the hardiest of religious images of man, this one has been as severely bruised as any in its career in the modern world. It survived the heavy storms which battered the traditional forms of the religious life from the fifteenth century on, but it had to take up life as part of philosophical system and lore. Thus biblical man was the darling of God. Created in the image of God, he was destined to endure divine judgment and finally to enjoy divine favor without stint. "Whom the Lord loveth he chasteneth [Heb. 12:6, KJV]"; the Maker of the heavens and the earth cares infinitely for his darling, so he will not always be angry, and in due season he will bless him with riches past imagining. But when the philosophical creators of the modern world could no longer embrace such an image, they were ready with conceptual surrogates. The Ego of the Cartesian system, Spinoza's intellectual lover of God, Kant's noumenal self, bodied forth as the rational moral agent who is entitled to hope for immortality, a perfection of happiness and virtue in a realm transcending the limitations of the world of space, time, and flesh—each in its own way makes man a special case in the cosmos.

The first half of the nineteenth century saw even greater triumphs for the human ideal. Now man stands forth as the crux of the world dialectical process. He is *microcosmos;* as he wags, so wags the world. Religious imagery having been overcome on the high plateaus of philosophic system, man's self-realization is just as firmly as ever believed to be the grand business of reality.

Then the storms broke, and the image of man as the darling and paradigm of the cosmic process was shattered. Darwinism sealed man back into the animal kingdom and made Chance king therein. Nietzsche proclaimed "God is dead!" and ripped the amiable religious disguises away from man's infinite capacities for deceit, resentment, and self-aggrandizement. Freud reduced the sense of the transcendent to an illusion at the far end of neurotic feeling-projections and piously scanned the future for an end to the sorry business. And two world wars have made it very easy to believe that the veneer of civilization is terribly thin and brittle. So the erstwhile darling is diminished to a naked ape whose capacities for hell-raising have latterly assumed a cosmic magnitude. In that respect alone man seems now to have transcendental properties.

The Victim. The successor of the Darling seems to be the Victim. This is the image of man trapped inextricably in a system. Whatever the system is, it destroys freedom, integrity, hope, dignity—in a word, humanity. If the system fails in this fell but purblind intent, it is as much an accident as a triumph of human courage or wit.

This image may not strike you as being wholly modern. Powerful expressions of the theme do certainly come to mind. There is Sophocles' Oedipus. Is he not a victim of a cosmic system, against the decrees of which he struggles in vain? But we cannot ignore the fact that in Sophocles' theology the cosmic system is committed to justice; or the equally compelling fact that Oedipus implicates himself in his fate. Moreover, Oedipus is made finally to stand as a ward of a special divine providence; the curse under which he lives and dies is intended to be a blessing for many.

A more likely candidate for Victim in the imagination of the ancient world is the figure of Pentheus in *The Bacchae* of Euripides. He is the earnest young man whose evangelical zeal for abolishing immoral and irrational religion arouses the fury of Dionysius, whose cult is the target of Pentheus' reforming passion. The radical theologian is destroyed by his own mother in a peculiarly horrible way. But brutal as it is to say so, Pentheus asked for his terrible fate. Indeed, in *The Bacchae* there is far less cosmic machinery to overtake overweening pride than in Sophocles' liturgical dramas, and far more emphasis on what we should call the dynamics of personality. Pentheus is truly a victim, but the way in which his character is his fate is supposed to be instructive to the beholder. "What he suffers, he suffers justly." From our lofty position in the moral universe we may lament that notion of justice. There are hints that old Euripides was not wholly happy with it.

And what about Job? There is a mighty image, but should we call him Victim? He is ground into the dust in a terribly systematic way. He is the capital figure of a man upon whom unmerited suffering is heaped up with a prodigality the book will not allow to be set down as accidental. But God never loses sight of him; and on his side of the strange transaction, Job holds fast to his integrity. In the end God provides ample evidence that Job is still his darling. This theological literary turn is an undying offense to modern theological wisdom.

Our world produced a variety of persuasive images of the Victim that have little connection with these great figures of the past. Here is Camus's Meursault, who can as easily be called the Victim as the Stranger. For him the deadly system is reality itself. It seduces man into loving and seeking happiness and then suspends the sword of death over every moment, so that every achievement of happiness is given a rotten heart. Here too is Hemingway's Frederic Henry of *A Farewell to Arms*. For him the First World War is the commanding symbol of the System: it is a monstrously random and reckless dealer of the cards of life, love, and death. With her last breath his beloved Catherine tells it like it is: "It's just a dirty trick." We remember, too, Heller's Yossarian of *Catch-22*. Again war and the military mind are symbolic condensations of a system of reality that is quite literally mad. Heller encourages us to laugh at Yossarian's antics, but we know all along that his dedicated program for living forever will not protect him from the knife. Are we uplifted at the end to realize that the System does not particularly care who gets it? If you can't win, what sort of fool is the man who keeps trying? Not in the same league with *The Idiot* of Dostoevski; but then, the mad Russian was religious.

So far the Victim does seem to have a sense of the transcendent. He is haunted by a boundary and a power he cannot pass through or effectively resist. But neither the limit nor the power of death adds anything of nobility, anything of meaningfulness. Death is simply the last and greatest of brute facts.

Kafka's rendition of the Victim is a somewhat different case. In his view the System had transcendental nuances running beyond random and unbeatable death. K (or Joseph K) cannot help believing that the System knows a good deal about him and has something in mind for him. He is therefore committed to cracking the secret. Like Job, he wants a fair hearing. Unlike Job, he never gets it. All he gets are cryptic signals from beyond. They do not save him from dying "like a dog."

These literary allusions are not intended to suggest that creative writers in our time are the only ones obsessed with the image of the Victim. The contemporary world reeks and reels with this image. Here is the man—his name is Legion—who sees himself trapped in the economic system. He is too thoroughly boxed in, buttoned down, tied up, overcommitted, and undermotivated to break out. The System has swallowed him whole, all that he is and ever hopes to be. Not even death carries the value of transcendence. It simply marks the end of the book in which every chapter is just more of the same old life. Life in the squirrel cage is just one damned thing after another. But who knows what it's like outside?

Thus are we led to represent ourselves as depotentialized and dehumanized by the massive structures and unremitting demands of society.

The Victim cries, "What can *I* do against such might and cunning? Nothing! So it is better for all concerned, for me and my loved ones, to adjust, fit in smoothly, and make no ripples."

This is a plausible plea. Secular society generates a powerful sense in the individual of being an easily replaceable part of a huge machine that has a will of its own. This is what we mean by the instrumentalizing of human life. We are hard pressed to find a loftier epitaph for the good citizen than "His was a useful life." In his natural lifetime, the Victim knows that he is used. He does not know that he is loved as a singular person, whether or not he is a good tool.

Where this sense of being depotentialized by the System prevails, personalistic religion surely has its work cut out. If the overpowering social system calls all the shots upon which my visible success in this world depends, how real can an appeal to a transcendentally wise, powerful, and solicitous God possibly be? He is often invoked as the divine friend of the System. Why should I think he has any interest in me if I am hostile to the System?

The Stranger. This image may seem somewhat less harsh than the Victim. Perhaps this is because it seems to grow out of a long and distinguished religious history. The ancient Israelite is enjoined to remember that he too was once an alien in a strange and heathenish land, and his father was a wandering Aramean. The Christian for many centuries saw himself as a pilgrim, a stranger in the world here below waiting to be summoned to his true and heavenly home, and in the meantime warned to be on guard against the wiles of the world, the flesh, and the devil.

No doubt these versions of the Stranger differed from each other in important ways. Nevertheless they made common sense against every cultural and psychological inducement to render ultimate loyalty to any social order that professed not to fear God and thus was free to dispose of human life as some human want might suggest. Thus these religious versions of the Stranger were both steeped in transcendental power; and they were both, therefore, able to generate acute discomfort in the hearts of those who did indeed bow the knee and submit the will to cultural gods.

The image of the Stranger has largely lost that power. Such discomposure as now grips the men of this age is no longer clearly related to a vision of a kingdom of messianic beauty grasped as the true homeland of the spirit. The Stranger is now likely to express one or the other of two strikingly different formations of alienation. The first of these is an alienation from self, brought on by anxiety about missing one's share of the goodies so lavishly displayed in our society. Many people seem to find something morally dubious about a man who does not perform— read *produce*—up to standard. The fact that he is missing out on some of the goodies packaged for men of his rank is ample proof that he is not doing his best. So he is condemned to live in a cloud of anxiety and self-accusation. If the nearest of kin and community do not add their reproaches to his own, he is unusually fortunate. "How *could* you think of settling down *here* when with proper effort from you we could live where we really belong?" Today for uncounted millions that is the existential question.

The other shadow cast by the Stranger is very different from this; it is indeed quite alienated from it. This is an idealistic recoil from the standard expectations and payoffs of the social system. It is a prophetic convulsion of disgust with the callousness toward the very misery produced by the system, and with the self-excuses and self-righteousness of the people who represent themselves as Victims of the system and yet pick off most of the goodies. This sense of shattering failure and a complementary anxiety lest restitution and amendment be delayed too long are the products of the intuited requirements of the ideal ethical commonwealth. Much of the power of this Stranger comes from his burning conviction that he is thus in touch with a transcendent realm of value. It is interesting that he is likely to reject the offices of traditional religion as in any way necessary for ascertaining what his forefathers would have called the perfect will of God. His *gnosis* of the real good is intuitive, personal, invincible, complete. He has been appointed to tear down the walls of the evil City of Man. Sometime after he has finished, persons of like purity may be able to build a blessed community in its place.

Here, then, is the image of the idealistic prophet who is a stranger by choice and transcendental vocation, a stranger in his own land and among his own people. Unkempt, girt about with leathern garb, fiery-eyed, ready with thunderous denunciation of a crooked and corrupt generation, he is decidedly not a reed quaking in the tepid blast of middle-class disapproval. Forearmed with sophisticated theories about ideology and class structure, he knows that every defense of the System is tainted with mortal corruption; and so every penitential gesture short of reaching for the blowtorch is phony.

I suggest that the unavoidable and so far unresolvable social phenomenon of the age, the shattering confrontation of adult and youth, is best understood as a violent conflict of images. The adult generations make much of the Victim, and particularly the Victim of the social system. They say, "We would have made the important changes, for we too dreamed dreams and saw visions of a better world for all. But the System in the end was too much for us. And now all we ask is a little understanding and some peace and quiet. Let now thy servant depart in peace. Anyway, what's so terrible about the General Motors way of life? It has kept you in college in creature comfort for lo these many moons." To which the prophetic Stranger makes reply, "In behalf of true humanity we spurn your good life of meaningless and expensive baubles. It stinks of hypocrisy and sellout. You ask for peace but seek to perfect the uses of violence. Your home is a prison, and you are trapped in it. Your church is a museum and a graveyard of high hopes, honest love, and humane faith."

There are doctrinal factors in this conflict, but they are secondary. There are philosophical arguments, but they are indecisive. The main thing is a brutal clash of images.

The Player. This image takes wings and flies to the antipodes, far, far away from the embattled scene just surveyed and perhaps from all the other images considered so far. For here man appears as the creature of make-believe. He draws out of imagination a world that never was on land or sea, and for nothing but his own delight.

Four elements of this image will bear inspection: (1) It is not an accident that man lives in a world created by imagination; (2) the make-believe world is able to take man into itself despite the commonsensical prejudice that the imaginary is subjective and private; (3) therefore the make-believe world is something into which man can escape either to avoid or to transcend the factual order of things; (4) the fictional world is intrinsically interesting and valuable, whether or not life in the factual order of things is directly improved by it.

1. Human creativity begins in and with the imagination, and this is the singular faculty for apprehending the nonexistent. Imagination grasps all the modalities of the contrary-to-fact: the not-here-but-elsewhere, the once-but-no-longer, the not-yet-but-sometime-coming. This is a remarkable power. The sense of the transcendent lives in it.

2. The make-believe world is able to internalize man; it can ingest him and thereby take him out of himself. For art this is the phenomenon of identification with a character of fiction. For religion this is the phenomenon of participation in a community that reaches back into

a past much deeper and richer than my individual past and opens out upon a future I shall never occupy in my own person.

3. Therefore I can plot a course that will carry me out of the agonies and blandishments of the factual order of things into a vastly richer world of make-believe. I can convert all or the gist of life into a game and confess that the rules thereof are set by a mysterious Player to whom the Game belongs, even though he may not appear in it in his own form. Thus one of the most persuasive summons to embrace harsh realistic duty is "Play up, man, and play out of the game!"

4. Enjoying the form and power of the Game, I may reasonably suppose that the factual order at its very best is only a part of it and quite the least significant part at that. The transcendent Player did that with his left hand. Why then should I treat the System with the deadly seriousness it ordains?

The secular spirit holds the make-believe in deathly serious suspicion. So the self-alienated Stranger is compelled to invent sober excuses for playing. And the prophetic Stranger is compelled to give his games a divinely explosive metaphysical warhead. In both cases we may begin to suspect that someone is taking hold of the factual order with the pincers of unstated dogma at the behest of uncriticized image. The dogma is that reality is a joyless affair. The image is that of man condemned to work incessantly at an impossible task in a strange and hostile land. Thus are the Victim and the Stranger jumbled together in a barbarous, unlovely package: an unholy marriage. No wonder the offspring look upon the Player as a man from Nowhere with a bag of implausible magic.

The Plastic Man. With this image we pass from the Modern to the Mod. It is the farthest out, and it is therefore the quintessentially contemporary.

The Plastic Man comes in two shapes. One is merely modern; he has, that is, some connections with earlier ages. We may call him Transitional Man. The other is mod; his connections are with the future. We may call him the Infinite Adapter.

Transitional Man is a creature linking an earlier state of human development and a later one. What he is in himself does not matter so much as his being a stage on the way to something better. So far this image has a connection with earlier representations of those generations of mankind which lived toward a consummation not available to them. "All these, though well attested by their faith, did not receive what was promised, since God had foreseen something better for us, that apart from us they should not be made perfect [Heb. 11:39-40]." The man who wrote this and the people for whom he wrote it believed that the time of consummation was at hand, and *they* were therefore not transitional; in them history was about to be fulfilled, not of themselves or for themselves but through God and for his glory. The modern image of Transitional Man has left these religious dimensions behind. Nietzsche is the great prophet of this change. That admirable creature he calls the Free Spirit is a "bridge to the future." And even of Superman, Nietzsche proclaims, "He exists to be overcome"—not, of course, by pygmies but by still greater realizations of creative power. The triumph of evolutionism forced an overcoming of Nietzsche's vision of Time as an eternal, self-enclosed circle. Thus Transitional Man faces a really open future. There is no end in sight because there is no end. But this means that man is not the end, either. He is not the cherished objective of some purpose, dim or bright, latent in the cosmic process. He is a happy accident, though no one else laughs.

So the connections Transitional Man has with eschatological man are not all that rich. The Darling has a future bright with glorious promise because God has his eye and his hand on him. Whether or not this creature has a home beyond the skies makes no difference to his status in the flow of history; his fulfillment is assured, and time has then an end. So eschatological man is grounded and crowned in transcendence. At the center of his being there is an invincible divine summons to seek a country where God is all in all, the perfecter of human life. For God is the potter, human life is his clay, and he is fashioning something beautiful in his own sight.

Transitional Man is not such a summons. He is a product of a creative élan wholly within nature which only in man knows the score and cares about the outcome. Only in man does Nature care. But can man's caring make a difference in the direction of the evolutionary process? Granted that Transitional Man is secular; he answers to no Outsider. Does he have the right as clearly as he has the power to change the genetic stock, to throw the switch and send humanity off on quite a different track in a trackless field of possibility?

The question is formidable. How can we answer it wisely unless we know what images of himself Transitional Man has? Does he cast himself in the role of Lord of all he surveys? Is he, rather, the pragmatic utilitarian Engineer, ready to build what others design? Or does he still contend with a desperate sense of being a servant of a higher purpose to which he must answer now for his intention and later for the far-flung consequences?

Transitional Man is not all the way out from under that transcendental sense. Plastic Man in his mod formation has made it: the Infinite Adapter. This is the image of man as sheer possibility.

The Infinite Adapter has radically reoriented the eschatological horizons of human existence. For him there is no single all-encompassing goal upon which all lines converge. Even death has been reoriented; it is something that happens to people who deserve it: the aged, the rigid, the structured. Otherwise it is a pointless accident, a cancellation of possibility rather than a possibility in the infinite field.

Personal identity also requires reorientation for the flowing purposes of the Infinite Adapter, the mod version of Plastic Man. He is by definition a multitude: I am many, not one or two. I am not what I was. I shall become, if I want, what I am not. That is the backward-forward plurality of the Infinite Adapter. There is also the lateral plurality: I am this and that and these and those and here and there, all at once. I am everything and nothing. I am on the road but not to anywhere in particular. Send not to ask who I am, because by the time you get through I will be something else.

The image of the Infinite Adapter is something more than the creature who rotates through a select number of life-styles, either in imagination or in the factual order. He is a being with many masks, each of which has as good a claim as any other to being authentic. But there is nothing behind the shifting masks except the will to be various. This and nothing else is the real I of the Infinite Adapter, this desire to play at being all things. The object of the play is not to deceive. The object is to taste the essence of the part, so far as this can be procured by projection rather than by condensation or concentration of self into one thing. Thus he does not stretch toward some form of existence that would be the ideal completion of destiny. He assumes that he will have time enough to enjoy the essence of the pluriform life. Beyond that lie the dismal plains of uniform existence, indistinguishable at the far edge from the motionless salt sea of death.

In his own sight, therefore, Plastic Man in his mod version is the maker and molder of his own pluriform life. That is the ideal. I think that the cultural realities are not unambiguous. The social system needed plastic, a cheap synthetic fabric adaptable to a multitude of purposes and without value or interest in itself. Thence to the metaphor: The System heats, twists, beats, massages, molds, synthesizes human life into an incredible variety of roles and functions, none of which has an intrinsic value or interest in itself. If we take the next step and construe the image of the System cybernetically, we can very well make the Prophetic Stranger a function of the System itself: that moment in its operation when a malfunction lights up a panel and circuitry sophisticated beyond all comparison with ancient magic begins at once to resolve the block, discharge the tension, and go on to glory.

Undoubtedly this image of the System is profoundly distasteful for the moment to the self-idealization of Plastic Man in his mod version. He sees himself as potent to make of himself anything he wants. He is the self-creating creature. And he is therefore, in his own image, perilously godlike. His essence is sheer possibility. Yet he lives in a system that will not admit that there is any possibility beyond its control.

Thus the latest image out stands in a puzzling relationship to the social system. The system needs a high degree of plasticity in its human constituents. Some of its constituents imagine that this plasticity is a metaphysical freedom with which they are mysteriously endowed. To others it seems to be the antithesis of freedom because it assumes a systematic right and power to manipulate human life without respect to ultimate ends. If, therefore, Plastic Man is the best the age can produce as the image of creative personal freedom, we may wonder whether the triumph of secularism is a solid victory for man.

Here then are samples from the bag of images we carry about as children of modernity. I have a final question to pose: Are images reformable? Or, put in religious terms: Is the imagination redeemable? In both forms the question assumes that reformation is or might be desirable. Many will deny that a reformation of images is now desirable. I suspect that many would deny that it is possible. In our time that is more likely to be a triumph of the social system than of metaphysical intuition and argument.

Let us take a case in point, and suppose that Plastic Man—or the Victim, for that matter—seems to us to be a deficient image. It strikes us, let us say, as clearly faithful to some aspects of our existence but it distorts others. Perhaps many people see themselves as plastic. But we say to them, "That's not good enough! You cannot really be all things, either in succession or simultaneously. If you are versatile, you can work and play at many things successfully. But that very bundle of diverse accomplishments is a product of high standards of performance rigorously applied by a self in command at the center. *That* is the real self, the real you; for without it your life would be a random clutch of interesting fragments."

I believe that this sermonette is fundamentally sound. We may nonetheless reasonably doubt that sermons, short or long, accomplish anything other than the self-vindication of the preacher when things go wrong on schedule. If they are to accomplish anything meatier, our sermons must also draw on viable and vivid images. Rail at Plastic Man if he arouses a holy ire. But do not expect him to wither under philosophical attack. He will yield ground, if not crown, to a more commanding image expressed and conveyed in fable, song, drama, dance, liturgy, through which some deep spring of humane passion is released.

"Some deep spring of humane passion" bespeaks a theological view of man: In the depths, at the core of his being, man is a creature of humane passions. This doctrine is a stranger in the councils of the learned today and an alien in the haunts of mod culture. In high and low places the ruling image of man is that of a creature loaded by nature with animal drives that must be tamed and transformed. That is the arduous and costly business of civilization. The ferocious paradox of civilization, on those terms, is clear indeed. The process of humanizing the naked ape may give him access both to instruments that geometrically augment his capability for destructiveness and to high-level principles justifying his exercise of this capability.

What are the images with which to oppose and best these low estimates of man? I think they are the cluster called the Player. There is the creature capable of spontaneous joy and sorrow. He can summon a world from the depths of his being as spirit and use it as a test of sanity of the factual order of things and, beyond that, as divining rod to probe for richer kingdoms than eye has yet seen. True, the Player is an illusionist. But he can set a play "to catch the conscience of a king." He can spin a yarn first to engross King David and then to spring the trap of awful guilt beneath his feet.

So I lament a world that makes preachers of clowns rather than clowns of preachers. I lament a world that insists on making laughter self-accusative and every tear a reflex of guilt. It is high time again to dance before the Lord, and not as a puppet jiggling madly on the end of the string but as a free spirit leaping in unbridled joy to greet the undying radiance of the Eternal.

Will that image stick? We may doubt it, saying, "It is too frivolous for a world so sick and tormented." So let us remember that man is not redeemed from sin and suffering by "the spirit of heaviness." He does not get on with his proper business in a mood of unrelenting self-seriousness.

Contemporary culture lays that mood upon us all. That is a major triumph of secularism as a paradoxically religious force. For if there is no one else to keep an eye on our interests, we cannot afford ever to close both eyes or even wink promiscuously. That is what I call self-seriousness.

I do not of course know whether the Player can cure this dis-ease of the spirit of modern man. Nonetheless, we should send for him.

7
The Ethics of Dissent

There are many ways of asking ethical questions about dissent. In this discussion I can only hope to touch clearly upon one or two issues, and not even dream of being either comprehensive or decisive. But to be clear even about one or two ethical questions, I find it necessary for myself to say what I mean by "dissent" in this discussion. So let us begin by agreeing that by dissent we have something more particular in mind than "disagreement," even though we might also agree that dissent is a kind of disagreement. But what kind? Can we not agree that dissent is refusal to accept a general agreement as binding upon oneself? In order to make more clear what we have in mind by dissent, let us add another factor that will, I trust, add the political-ethical quality we are looking for. *That further factor is refusal to accept a general agreement upon policy designed and executed for the general welfare.* For the purpose of the views I shall consider, it does not make very much difference whether the general agreement determines the policy in question or is given to the policy once it is enunciated by the leadership of the state.

Before going any further, let us be as clear as possible about the ethical status of "general agreement" in a democratic society. Hardly anyone is likely to say (that is, say sincerely) that general agreement is either the definition or the criterion of the rightness of a principle or a policy. Yet there is a very strong sentiment that a general agreement is binding upon all and not merely upon those who go to make it up as a general agreement. The consequence can be very simply stated: The dissenter is morally bound not to act against the general agreement even though he believes that the general agreement is wrong. For the moment let the accent fall on *act* rather than upon *think* or *speak*, simply because

This chapter is reprinted with permission from *Theology Today*, XXIII, No. 4 (Jan. 1967), pp. 496-504.

our democracy recognizes the sovereign right of the individual to think and to speak as he pleases.

Permit me to note in passing that I have not said that the dissenter is *in fact* so bound morally, but only that this is a consequence of the sentiment, so central to our society, that "the majority rules." I ask you to note this because it will help us to get on to the ethical issues of dissent.

I

Now I want to put a question that will sound more psychological than philosophical (or logical), even though that is not the way I intend to use it. Why would one hold out against the general agreement? Here we are not asking about the motives of the dissenter—and that is why I say that the question is not a psychological one. Rather, we are asking about his reasons. Asking that question, we can certainly expect the following answer from the dissenter: "I reject the policy (or principle) to which there is general agreement because I believe that the policy is wrong." From this statement we proceed to draw a perfectly proper (and, indeed, necessary) inference: The dissenter believes he knows what is right, at least in this case (the case of a particular policy).

We ought to proceed thence to another inference, to which as a rule we shall have been preceded by the dissenter himself: Since the dissenter believes he knows what is right in a given case, he has a moral obligation to communicate what he believes he knows. (I suspect in fact that we could agree, majority and dissenters alike, on a kind of axiom on which the Good Society is based: One owes it to that society, and not merely to oneself, to communicate what one believes to be right and good for that society.)

So now we must put another question to the dissenter, and again it would be unfortunate if this question were taken to be primarily psychological. *Why do you believe that you are right and the general agreement is wrong?* I expect that he would answer as follows: "I know what is really good for our society (and perhaps for humanity as well), and therefore I have a sound basis for dissent from the general agreement on a given policy." In framing his answer this way, we have of course simply assumed his rationality. Any given dissenter might want to make a more modest answer for himself, such as: "I just *feel* that the general agreement is wrong."

This is certainly much more modest. Unfortunately, it is one of the answers that we know in advance is wrong. Or perhaps it would be fairer to say misplaced rather than wrong, since what we mean to tell him is that our question is about the *justification* for his dissenting action and not about its explanation. We assume that he would not endorse such a doctrine as: One ought to do whatever one feels.

Let me summarize the situation down to this point, in this way. The dissenter is appealing to what he knows of the good for our society (and/or for humanity as such) as justification for his dissenting action. We ought, therefore, to be ready for a rather different question: *How do you know this good?*

II

The novelty of this question can be learned empirically as well as logically. Empirically we are likely to learn that dissenters fall rather promptly into two quite distinct classes, just so soon as this question comes up in a serious way.

Class A. These dissenters claim that the knowledge of the good necessary to make assessments of policy and principle is generally available to anyone who will go to the trouble to learn the facts and to think about them in the light of the rational good. Class A thereupon itself breaks down into two subgroups.

A-1: The "rational good" is a fancy way of referring to this society's fundamental ethical principles; thus the dissenter who says that our nation is *in principle* committed to a revolutionary ideal, and who thereafter dissents because he sees our actual policies as being consistently antirevolutionary, as in Southeast Asia, and perhaps also in Alabama. Like the rest of us, he may have made some loose and otherwise unwarranted assumptions about revolution. And, again like the rest of us, he may be wrong about the facts concerning any given revolution. (An illustration of the first: Is it really the case that 1776 in America, 1789 in France, 1917 in Russia, 1848 in Germany, and 1936 in Hungary are all so many realizations of the Revolutionary Ideal? An illustration of the second: Is the Viet Cong an internal revolutionary thrust or is it a "foreign invasion" using native personnel?)

A-2: The "rational good" is transnational and transethnical and perhaps transhistorical; that is, the "rational good" is not defined by or limited to "self-interest" of the state or of the person or of the social class. Thus we have the dissenter who contends that the general agreement is wrong, whether or not it is consistent with this nation's fundamental ethical principles. Some Christian dissenters clearly fall into this group, and especially those dissenters for whom "Christian" is largely a synonym for the best we know by the exercise of our rational powers.

Class B. There are dissenters who claim that the knowledge of the good necessary to make sound assessments of policy and principle is *not* available to just anyone who will go to the trouble to learn the facts and to think about them in the light of the rational good. Class B at once breaks down into three subgroups. (In the contemporary situation, these subgroups have constructed a whole series of uneasy political-tactical alliances.)

B-1: The knowledge of the real good is available to those alone to whom God has revealed (or is revealing) his will. Empirically the sum total of these persons is very small, at least at the present moment in our society; but dissenters of B-1 stripe have a theological explanation of this fact (the doctrine of election). Thereafter the B-1 dissenter must make up his mind whether to seek control of the State, despite the general agreement against him, on the grand assumption that the godly and righteous man ought to be in charge of affairs. To do this, however, he would have either to work to change the general agreement in his favor, in which case he would cease being a dissenter, or to seize power by violence or deceit or both. I think it can be shown empirically that when B-1 dissenters do become active revolutionaries, they are likely to claim that their own violence and/or deceit is divinely ordained. Theologically this is different from the doctrine that the end justifies the means. It does not strike me as being an ethical improvement upon that doctrine.

B-2: The knowledge of the real good is available only to those who are able to strip their minds and hearts of the last vestige of loyalty to the structures and principles of capitalist society and thereafter accept the dogmas of dialectical materialism and the discipline of the Communist party leadership. There is an interesting difference between B-1 and B-2, and the difference is essentially theological. B-2 believes, I suppose, that anyone *could* put himself in this position. B-1 believes that only God can do (or has done) this. Yet B-2 also agrees that in our society the number of those who really know the good is very small. But B-2 has a socioeconomic explanation for this situation—that is, a strictly naturalistic-materialistic theory—which he calls "scientific" and the rest of us are likely to call "metaphysical." And also, like B-1, the Communist revolutionary knows perfectly well that he could take command of this society only by violence and deceit. Also like B-1, he has no real hope of assuming command here in the early future. Also like B-1, he believes that a time is coming when his dissent will be perfectly vindicated. With

B-1, B-2 knows that in the meantime even this hope is hidden from the vision of the unregenerate majority.

It would be crassly irresponsible on our part, even in this sketch, to pass over silently one of the striking differences between B-2 and B-1. B-1 is systematically committed to thinking and talking about the good and the real good in undisguised ways. Even if he believes religiously that no ethical appeal can be made against the revealed will of God, he also believes that the real and final good is made available in that revelation. On the other hand, B-2 is systematically committed to use all ethical talk tongue-in-cheek, since he does not believe that history is made by persons acting out their moral convictions. B-2 does of course believe that a truly good state of affairs will someday be achieved for what is left of humanity after imperialistic wars have ended once and for all, and after Communist-inspired revolutions have taken their last toll of flesh and blood. Moreover, he is for the present quite prepared to justify his revolutionary dissent by appealing to the doctrine many of us were brought up to believe is properly jesuitical, "The end justifies the means." But again the difference: The end is determined by mechanical causes, not by ethical aspiration.

B-3: The knowledge of the real good is available only to those who are already living, so far as the practicalities will allow, beyond all the illusory comforts of dogma and moral convention. (If we wish to use conventional terminology, B-3 is the *anarchistic* dissenter.) Again B-3 recognizes, or even insists, that his kind of dissent is likely to be a numerical minority and may, in fact, be diminishing. The explanation of this can easily be found in the character of the good that this B-3 dissenter knows. The good he claims as his lodestar is *freedom*. As we should expect, this is freedom from something and freedom for something. It is freedom from artificial restraints, and all moral conventions and dogmas are judged to be artificial rather than merely arbitrary. It is freedom for creativity, and creativity is very largely understood as self-expression; and self-expression is more a matter of being oneself than of fashioning or ordering something. B-3, in other words, is quite suspicious of freedom as at last being able "to make a contribution" and of doing things *in order* to, or with a view to, doing something else. And from this alone it ought to be quite clear why B-3, too, defines his values as over against the general agreement. General agreements run toward structure; and structures generate conventions, rules, laws, etc. To this degree he is a rebel rather than a revolutionary. Revolutionaries hope someday to run things. The rebel knows that that way lies damnation.

III

Both empirically and dialectically, dissent presupposes the general agreement and a relatively settled state of affairs. I want in this section to raise a question about the relation of dissent to the "relatively settled state of affairs." Specifically, I want to ask what justifies acceptance of its protection and appropriation of its resources for the purposes of dissent in the forms in which we have been discussing it. (I am of course talking about bona fide Americans in the American situation.)

So far as I can see, all types of dissenters claim the following rights and privileges made possible only by a relatively stable society.

1. Protection of the highest positive law, whether or not that law is congruent with the true and real good. If it is the case that the law is made for the good of the people as a whole, it is hard to see how this claim could be faulted. A citizen does not forfeit his basic rights simply because he dissents actively from the general agreement on public policy, provided that his dissent does not take the form of violating a capital law. If he makes himself an exception to such law, it is hard to see why he should claim its protection or whatever benefit it allows or grants.

2. Access to the processes, both formal and informal, by which policy is determined; or, if not determined in a particular instance, at least held open to modification. Here it is assumed that since policy, like law, is or ought to be for the good of all, free and open discussion of it is a requirement of the health of this society. Actually, we have been thinking of dissent that acts against a policy already in force rather than one not yet in force. The principle appears to be the same, however—namely, that the right kind and volume of dissent may lead to a modification of policy, and this for the general welfare rather than simply for the good of the dissenter.

3. Opportunity to seek power through the regular channels, formal and informal, provided by the law and custom of the land; and this with a view to changing the policies of the land.

All these claims are justified by the assumption that the basic structures of law, order, and due process are the common property of the whole people. They are justified also by the assumption that policy ought to be formulated on the basis of the broadest familiarity with the facts and after all viewpoints have been expressed. This second assumption is a weak one for Class B dissenters, since they do not believe that knowledge of the good is generally available. If Class B dissenters nonetheless insist on this second assumption, I should think it would be for tactical rather than for substantive reasons.

But what are we to say about the dissenters, of whatever class, who do not actually accept the fundamental ethical principles upon which our society is built? I suggest that our answers to this question ought to depend upon what the antiprinciple dissenter is really attempting to accomplish in his dissent.

Let us suppose (a) that such a dissenter belongs to Class A. What he may be attempting in his dissent is to bring enough people to their senses to adopt principles, as well as policies, more congruent with the rational good. By "rational" good, such a dissenter will almost certainly mean the good for humanity as such. He may believe that this nation is ethically superior to any other de facto state of affairs but yet needs great and profound alteration. Or he may believe that some other nation is our ethical superior, but since he is here rather than there he will do the best he can with us, not as a servant of that better state but as a servant of the rational good.

Let us suppose (b) that an antiprinciple dissenter belongs to Class B. I should suppose that wherever he belongs in the subtypes he ought to be either a revolutionary or a nonparticipant where his nonparticipation will have the most symbolic striking power.

This brings us to two final questions. Can the Class B dissenter to the fundamental principles of the nation consistently claim the same three rights clearly open to dissenters of the Class A type? I do not believe that he can do this consistently, but we can hardly doubt that he does in fact make these claims. This may be because he believes that he is American by accident of birth. But this of course confers duties as well as rights. In any case he has every right to be treated as a human being. But this is not in question. The question is whether as a human being living within these structures of law and custom he has a right either to attempt to undo those structures or to abdicate from their duties while claiming their rights.

Our last question takes off from this: What should those who participate in the general agreement do about the dissenters? Surely our answer to this depends on what we think the dissenter is up to and from what base he operates. Dissent which concurs with principle but disagrees with policy is surely a healthy symptom. Let us put it even more strongly. Dissent which grounds its disagreement with policy upon a good higher than traditional principle and is yet a good to which we all have access, if we would make ourselves available to it, must surely be viewed as one of the potentialities of the moral development of the whole community. For even the most conservative among us cannot seriously suppose that tradition is a *definition* of the real good even if we suppose that it is a valid *criterion* of the real good. The tradition can be improved upon. It is the function of certain kinds of dissent to remind us of that great truth.

On the other hand, dissenters of Class B types clearly have upon them the burden of proof to certify their loyalty to country whatever their philosophical disagreements with its principles, so long as they wish to claim its rights and privileges. Frankly, I do not see how they can do this consistently. In the same vein I do not see how consistently we can accord them the basic rights and privileges of citizenship unless we can be reasonably sure of their inconsistent loyalty. We may, of course, all be saved by our inconsistencies; but that makes a very poor bet.

IV

I have not discussed the kind of dissent which assumes that the general agreement is actually a demonic conspiracy intent upon pillaging the wealthy and selling the country out to a diabolical enemy. In terms of labels we should have to call this the dissent of the Radical Right. The leadership of this minority group is either afflicted with severe paranoidal symptoms or cultivates such illness in its constituency. That is the reason that I have not discussed it in this context. Its proper discussion falls within the pathology of the body politic rather than within its philosophy. The forms of dissent I have discussed all assume rationality in their subjects and in the body politic; some, of course, more than others. So long as a dissenter is beyond conviction of error, either in forms of argument or substantively, he belongs to pathology.

Moreover, I have not attempted to assess the strengths or weaknesses of the theological and philosophical assumptions undergirding the various forms of dissent. To do so would carry us into theological convictions and metaphysical theories no one of which seems to me to throw indispensable light on the ethical-political phenomenon of dissent, except for persons who are already under theological conviction or subscribe to some metaphysical theory.

8
Man's Use of Power

There are three parts to this chapter. In the first I consider the general question of what is to be gained by clarifying fundamental categories. In the second part the concept of power as a category of political thought is considered. In the third part I ask what is meant by the moralization of power.

I

What is to be gained by clarifying fundamental categories? Many philosophers in the present scene would consider this question jejune and otiose. As they view their trade, it is largely dedicated to conceptual analysis; and the concepts they analyze (or, more generally, the "languages") are by no means those in which philosophy has a proprietory stake, if indeed there are any such concepts and language. It is axiomatic in linguistic philosophical circles that philosophy has no problems of its own, and from this we might reasonably conclude that it has no language of its own. One hears of people in the universities who say that a department with no business of its own has no business maintaining itself as a department. I hope that none of my readers entertains such surly sentiments.

Now, from behind the armor plate of invincible ignorance, I report the following answers to the otiose question before us.

1. One of the most ancient, honorable, and persistent aims of philosophy is the attainment of lucidity. Socrates says that the unexamined life is not worth living. Descartes makes clearness and distinctness of ideas the hallmarks of truth. Philosophers in the seventeenth and eighteenth centuries dedicate themselves to the improvement of understanding. Today even the philosophers who insist that "clarity is not enough" do not mean to obscure its importance.

But what is lucidity? Socratic wisdom sees it as a brightness of self-understanding that banishes the shadowy involutions of self-deception and penetrates the shield of ignorance. That mind is lucid which is unshuttered and thus enables its possessor to see himself and the world as they are. Philosophers today are more likely to suggest that lucidity is that quality of language which allows one to see what is intended in its use. Where discourse is fixed upon ideas, lucidity enables one to see how this idea rather than that is intended in a given sentence (or paragraph, chapter, etc.).

It may seem artificial if not perverse not to link lucidity as a persistent aim of philosophy with rationality. I throw myself on the mercy of the court with the simple plea that "rationality" would put us into a bigger and looser game. Eventually I hope to make an envious but civil gesture or two at it.

How is lucidity attained? An ancient and recently rejuvenated view holds that philosophy is a therapy designed to relieve the mind of defects so ingrained in it by successive cultural epochs as to make them seem metaphysical: the darkness of ignorance, the dimness of opinion both conventional and idiosyncratic, the confusion circling around pseudo-problems fostered by the systematic misuse of language. The redemption of the mind from these melancholy servitudes is a formidable task.

2. One such defect is the confusion engendered and sustained by the misuse of concepts. The history of science offers many illustrations of this. Of these, one of the most monumental was the application of categories of moral agency, such as intention, purpose, and aim, to all the phenomena of nature. As moral agents we know directly what we are talking about and what we mean to say when we use such concepts. No doubt there are satisfactions in imputing Purpose to Nature in all her ways, but these ascriptions defy direct verification; and the theoretical structures—the hypotheses ad hoc—necessary to support them eventually became incredibly complicated. In fact the progress of science in the modern world has depended very largely on restricting explanation to antecedent efficient linear causality. Nature rendered purposeful is Nature sadly confused.

A matching set of confusions is produced along the reverse route by applying concepts useful in natural science, such as mechanical patterns of causation, to human actions and interactions. Man rendered mechanical is man sadly abused.

It is not seriously to be doubted that important cognitive gains have been made traveling in both directions along this route. Nonetheless, confusions are encouraged by failing to see how important for both the *as though* concept is. Thus organic phenomena can be viewed as though they were teleologically related. Some aspects and elements of human behavior can be viewed as though they were mechanically interrelated. But metaphysical appetites—formidable indeed when disguised as something else—are not born to honor or obey such hygienic concepts as these *as thoughs*.

Thus the desire to render experience and the world intelligible throughout powerfully tempts us to convert metaphors into concepts and concepts into reality-valid doctrines. When the poet says, "O, 'tis love and love alone the world is seeking," we are not confused by *love*, though we may not wholeheartedly endorse the sentiment. When the ancient philosopher declares that the cosmic elements are held together by love, so long as the cosmos is in an integrative mood, and they are repelled by hatred when disintegration is the order of the day, we assume that *love-hate* is a metaphor in which a doctrine of attraction-repulsion is represented; but the metaphor leaves us fishing confusedly, fishing for other possibilities in speculative seas fifty thousand fathoms deep.

More modern illustrations of metaphor conversion are not hard to find. Here is Leibniz, certainly one of the most fertile of modern thinkers, who says that the elementary particles are centers of *feeling*. Here also is Whitehead, with a very similar doctrine. Are we to suppose that *feeling* is a metaphor? No; it is a category with a base in immediate self-experience (who does not know what it means to *feel?*), but it is infinitely generalizable, as categories must be. But then we need instruction on how much of the metaphor is retained. We need also a rule to guide the process of metaphor conversion; without it, confusion is licensed.

There is also such a thing as being trapped in a metaphor—if that metaphorical expression is allowable. Ordinary discourse is full of transitions from literal uses of a concept to metaphorical and analogical uses. These transitions are not always confusing by any means. Consider the following sequence:

   i. Daddy's *seat* is in the front row.
   ii. Washington is the *seat* of the nation.
   iii. The bowels are the *seat* of compassion.
   iv. The brain is the *seat* of the mind.
   v. "Heaven is my throne/And the earth is my footstool."

A young child might be puzzled by the transition from seat (i) to seat (ii), but the rest of us are not. The people of the Old Testament, or some of them at any rate, probably believed that seat (iii) was as literally true as seat (i). We are not likely to be confused by (iii) because we recognize this seat as a metaphor very similar to current vernacular: a "gut reaction." Seat (v) is clearly a poetic metaphor, and I should think the chances are very good that its author knew that, too. Seat (iv) has had a long history in metaphysics both conscious and unconscious as a concept rather than as a metaphor. One version of this is available in the wonderful aphorism of an eighteenth-century French philosopher: "The brain secretes consciousness as the liver secretes bile." I think this is a handsome illustration of being trapped in a metaphor. It is hard indeed to squeeze anything out of it except confusion.

I should not want to be understood as suggesting that conceptual clarity is rationally bound to clear away all the great questions of traditional metaphysics, such as the mind-body question. The point is much more modest: It is reasonable for the rest of us to ask any kind of systematic thinker, whatever his department, whether he can give us the rules explaining the linguistic conversions in his system. The conversion of metaphors into concepts is only one of them. There are also conversions of ordinary terms into highly specialized ones, often by stipulative definitions. Again, there is no objection in principle to stipulative definitions, but the burden of proof is not upon us if we say that these rearrangements of concepts fail to render experience lucid and the world intelligible.

Before leaving this matter of category confusion and the importance of reducing its empire, I want to delineate two petitions for exemption from the demands of conceptual clarity. One is theological; the other is ethical. Since it is important to put first things first, we begin with the theological.

Some theologians say that God is the *cause* of everything that exists and of everything that happens. From this it is clear that they intend to interpret God as the only real causal agent there is. Thus it would seem that everything happens because God causes it to happen, as any strict necessitarian would say, whether or not he was partial to using "God" as a word for the mechanical perfection of the cosmic system. But now there are theologians who say that some things happen not because God necessitates them but simply and purely because God permits them to happen. We can see how one causal factor among others might give place to some other such factor in a given situation. But God is not one causal factor among others; he is the only real cause there is. So it must be that the category of cause defies the demands for clarity in this instance. Perhaps there is some religious interest that cannot otherwise be properly served. It is not the business of the critic to assume the burden of proof for that.

There are also ethical interests that might well compel a systematic thinker to enter a plea for exemption from conceptual clarity. Suppose, for instance, that as a metaphysician I say: "By *determination* I mean the way in which everything happens of necessity from an infinitely complex set of antecedent causes." But then in another context I say: "We must *determine* to eliminate the causes of unnecessary suffering." "Determination" in the second instance speaks to a different interest, and it says a different thing. Moral agency is falsified or trivialized in the first instance. In the second instance moral agency is regarded as self-evidently real and as decisive.

I do not mean to suggest that all inconsistencies in theories or doctrines might be eliminated by a proper therapy or hygienic use of concepts. On the other hand, it is possible that clearing up conceptual confusions might help to bring into view, if not effectively realize, a greater degree of harmony among the interests of the self and the interests of society.

The first part of this chapter concludes with a cautionary note: Let us not confuse efforts to clarify concepts with the academic vice of insisting that every serious discussion begin by defining terms. Those efforts are awesomely infertile, as a rule. They produce acrimonious charges of "arbitrary!" "high-handed!" "woolly-headed!" and similar manifestations of fraternal affection.

Nonetheless, there is something to be said for this academic vice. The interests of a systematic discipline are poorly served by conceptual muddles. Indeed, a discipline can hardly be called systematic unless those muddles are cleared up or unless some powerful interest of the subject matter demands the perpetuation of conceptual ambiguity. (The complementary thesis in physics is not apposite here. Physicists know what they mean by "particle" and "wave." The defenders of the thesis say that the explanation of light requires both concepts.) But it is also true that important confusions are rarely cleared up helpfully by deploying fresh troops of stipulative definitions. A more excellent way consists of asking what range of experience is in fact engaged or solicited by a given concept. When a clear answer to that question is available, the experts can decide whether systematic inquiry needs to limit the range of that concept. In any case they had better decide upon signals for field variance in the use of a concept, if field variance is likely.

II

What can we make of power as a category of political thought? The concept of power is troubled by a variety of things, of which one of the most perplexing is the valuational ambiguity surrounding its use. Conventional views of politics see power as a brute reality largely immune to moralization. Popular wisdom has made Acton's famous dictum part of its canonical scriptures. It is axiomatic that the more power a person or a social collective has, the more difficult it becomes to make either responsive to ethical principle.

Such views have been given the dignity of sophisticated theorizing. Classical Marxian thought makes short shrift of ethical language for any but purely rhetorical purposes. Other forms of realpolitik may be less doctrinaire, but they agree on the amorality of power.

So perhaps it would be wise to divest the concept of power of its thin value load and use it as a counter in a system of mechanical (nonteleological) causality. We do not need to be reminded that this can be done in the mode of *as though*. But then there is the reverse route of the *as though*. Conventionally we hold the wielders of power responsible for their uses of it quite as though they were still moral agents, despite all the panoply of high office and monarchical postures, and quite as though power, the substance of their concerns and the joy of all their desiring, were no more recalcitrant to moralization than is traffic in buttons and bananas.

I suggest, therefore, that we reserve judgment on the clarity and validity of such *as though* concepts until we have looked further into the concept of power.

1. The concept of power often functions as a logical "primitive"; that is, as a foundational category. Where this is the case, failure to define power is predictable, since no definition of a primitive term is possible; its meaning must be caught in its use, and one of its functions is to provide the foundation of a systematic inquiry. Thus from the study of politics one would hope to learn how power is attained, how it is preserved, and how it is lost. One would be ill-advised to approach the study of politics with the expectation of learning what power is. One might as well go hat in hand to learn from biology what life is, or to physics to learn what matter is.

2. Though power may be a logical primitive in a systematic inquiry, other primitives are conceivable, such as justice and the general good. It does not follow, and it is not the case, that no definition of such concepts is possible; but none can be given in a system that uses them

as primitive concepts. Depriving them of definition and leaving them on the intuitive level may seem unpardonably arbitrary, in fact. It is also a fact that every system of explanation rests on primitives intuitively grounded or on stipulative definitions.

3. The concept of power is not necessarily a logical primitive. It may be derived from other concepts, such as authority and force.

4. Whether or not the concept of power is derived from the concepts of authority and force, it seems to compound or unite them otherwise. Moreover, it does not seem to be reducible to either of them except on pain of confusion. The power of a state is its ability to enforce its demands upon its own citizens and upon other states when that is necessary. But rulers and their advocates commonly claim that these demands are legitimated by considerations other than superior fire-power. There are many such warrants adduced for the exercise of power both in politics and in the lives of individual moral agents.

5. A moral principle may be a warrant for the exercise of power by a state against another state. Suppose, for example, it is said that A ought to be opposed because it is the author of great mischief for B. It might turn out that nothing could be done about A except to express moral condemnation of it; that is, "nothing could be done" because the risks of doing anything toothier seemed unacceptably high. Thus Henry Stimson discovered in the course of the Far Eastern crisis of 1931-32 that nothing could be done by this country to Japan except roundly to condemn the immorality of her behavior. He admitted that this represented the last recourse and was a confession of powerlessness. Perhaps he conceded too much there if, as he felt, one of the objectives of that moral censure was the creation of a climate of opinion hostile to international brigandage. Grant that a nation rarely mends her ways simply because others hurl moral censures at her. Nonetheless, the sinner may pause to reflect when she realizes that those censures are actually certificates licensing the application of force sufficient to restrain her, or perhaps even to destroy her. A good bit here depends on whether moral censure is only an acknowledgment of powerlessness or, to the contrary, is such a license. The fact that nobody is at the moment ready to pull the trigger does not ease anxiety so long as the gun is loaded and is aimed properly.

6. It has been argued ever since ancient times that the concept of authority as right to rule is reducible without remainder to superior force available to make the will of the ruler unbrookable. This venerable doctrine is haunted by logical oddities when it is applied to interpersonal

relations. After we have reviewed two of those, we shall have to ask (7) whether logical confusions also hound the doctrine when it is applied to the relations of states to one another.

i. If I say "might makes right," I have to explain what "right" means. If it is merely another way of spelling "might," I ought to say so. On the other hand, I may mean by "right" that people endowed with might, from whatever source, are entitled to the prerogatives of power, whatever they are. But whatever are they? Well, who determines that? The high and the mighty answer: "We do, of course; who else?" But suppose that the low and the powerless throw in their lots with one another and then proceed to undo the ruling class altogether and ensconce themselves in the seats of the mighty. Have the "rights" of the former rulers been violated? Hardly. Having no might now, they have lost their rights. No doubt they will resent this deplorable situation, but what *moral* weight can their complaints carry? Thus Nietzsche pours the acids of contempt over the multitudinous "mass men" who have so effectively haltered and hamstrung those whom Nature intended to prevail. But a man from that loathsome mass would have a bit of a point if he replied, "Well, then, Nature goofed originally or she blinked while we destroyed the giants in the earth."

The larger point is not that the theory cannot be consistently applied. Nor is it that few have the stomach to put the cold comfort of logical consistency ahead of unbroken and unthreatened enjoyment of power. The point is that we have only a logically odd sentence and not a theory at all until the conceptual confusion of "might" and "right" is cleared up.

ii. If I say to a bully, "You have no right to beat me up," he will probably reply, "That won't stop me." That may be painfully true, but stopping him from beating me up is only part of the reason for telling him that what he threatens to do is wrong. Another and larger reason is to justify, though not necessarily to inspire, a certain kind of retribution. But there is more: I should certainly like to have him consider the consequences of his behavior for himself, and I should like him also to propose a justification for it. The latter is not necessarily an appeal to his "conscience"—he may not have much there. It is an invitation to him to consider himself a moral agent; for the time will come when he will have to offer a moral justification for his actions or be judged an incompetent, subrational creature.

The bully may thereupon give me two black eyes instead of the one of the original project in order to prove that he is the boss of the block and to hell with my preaching. So Japan went her way in 1931-32, proving that she could get away with it—for so long as she could get away with it. Perhaps her biggest mistake was taking on Number One in December 1941. But why should we be reluctant to say that the whole adventure beginning with the first shots in the railyard in Mukden in 1931 was morally wrong? Perhaps because we do not want to make the egregious mistake of supposing that historical outcomes themselves establish moral culpability. It is bad enough to be a big loser. It is surely worse to be branded a criminal for having gambled and lost.

7. Heads of state often use the language of moral outrage in describing the actions of other nations. No doubt this is often designed for domestic consumption. That does not rule out the possibility that national leaders and the great masses of the people may alike firmly believe that there is a moral order overarching the nations of mankind. That piety may be misled as well as misleading. Is there any science capable of showing that it is misled, that it is inescapably illusory? History has many horror stories about how terribly misleading such pieties can be. But why are we reluctant to see these as tales of the infinitely varied ways in which rulers and peoples have misconstrued the requirements of the moral order?

One answer to that question is that politics at every level reveal a settled disposition in rulers to couch prudential warrants in ethical language, and a matching disposition in the perceptive populace to discount the ethical tone and interpret the appeals to prudence as so many exercises in expediency.

These plain historical truths invite a revision of the might-makes-right doctrine. We might want to propose now that all ethical imperatives are curiously disguised expressions compounded of interests ("I want x") and prudential prescriptions ("so I had better do a rather than b or c"). It is not necessary to say "interest makes right," because people often misread their own interests; and they often do such monumentally stupid things in trying to fulfill an interest that the whole show is botched. Still, these harsh facts do not alter the logic of the matter. That is a matter of seeing to it that "right" means fittingness, appropriateness and efficacy in the steps taken to fulfill an interest. The theory assumes that interests as such do not need justification.

But why should persons and peoples need to disguise their interests behind the concepts of ethical discourse? Prima facie, "I ought" does not feel anything like "I want." The logical function of "I ought" is just as clearly different from that of "I want." The latter simply records a psychic fact, an event in one's personal history, and as such it is not even remotely the beginning of a reason for anything. "I did *x* because I wanted to" identifies a cause but not a reason. "I ought" also records a psychic fact, but it and it alone is responsive to the moral *Why?* That question calls for the statement of a reason rather than an identification of a motive. What is at stake is *justification,* not *explanation.*

The theory here has precipitated another *as though* projection: It is as though persons were moral agents but in fact they are not.

It would be a strange fact that could establish this. Such oddities are not hard to find. They are of the order of psychic (and cultural) constraints and inducements to represent human life as entirely predictable in principle. "In principle" is a concession of current limitations of knowledge rather than admission of defect in outlook.

What is particularly odd about this *as though* concept is that it is construed as the demand of rationality. It is hard to resist the conclusion that we need to look elsewhere for a clearer concept of rationality. I do not intend to resist it.

8. It is not necessary to go to the Hesperides to find such a concept. Nor is it necessary to resort to stipulation. A clearer concept of rationality is visible in a common pattern of ethical argument, and it is commonly there as an assumption: Ethical appeals (appeals to an order of Ought) without determinate sanctions are deficiently rational. They are corrupted by impracticality. Here is our bully again. If there are no determinate sanctions available to make him regret his felonious ways, my telling him "You've no right to punch me in the eye" is not only an exercise in futility, it is irrational as well. To tell him that right is on my side and wrong on his is a rhetorical gesture unless there is an efficacious way of enforcing the distinction as well as drawing it. Otherwise the bully, if he is but normally perspicacious, will see that my rhetoric is calculated to cheat him out of what he regards as a legitimate satisfaction.

So there is a very small but real modicum of truth in Stalin's cynical remark, "God is on the side which has the greater number of divisions," however surprised we may be to discover theological wisdom in that quarter. There is little or no virtue in claiming to be right though entirely impotent. For if it is true that the rightness of a cause is not determined by counting the number of divisions, it is also true that there is something distinctively wrong in substituting a sense of being right for the actuality of being strong. It is the wrongness of irrationality.

I do not mean to suggest that there is inevitably something fishy about appealing to the moral order as such or to the verdict of history. Yet it may be useful to keep in mind that an appeal to the moral order may be an exercise in the self-justification of powerlessness. Moreover, answers from the moral order are notoriously slow in arriving, and they are often so Delphic as to be infinitely adjustable to the actualities. So appeals to the verdict of history are never far behind appeals to the moral order. But the verdicts of history are rendered by historians, and the axes they grind are in the main easily distinguishable from the sword of the blind Goddess.

9. There is another and quite different concept of rationality available in the ethical-political world. It is visible and potent in the realm of contracts, commitments, treaties, etc. It is the concept of *promise*. Here are some of its salient features and functions.

i. A promise creates an enforceable claim; it can be enforced upon its giver or maker. And the clearer it is that the promise is made in freedom, the more enforceable it becomes.

ii. What do we mean by "enforceable claim"? Specific answers to this question depend upon specific contexts of life and discourse, but there is a persistent general answer: Promise creates a relationship that cannot be arbitrarily destroyed or evacuated by the maker of the promise. There is, of course, a flat sense in which a contract freely proposed and entered into by the party of the first part can be freely broken by him. That is exactly the sense in which the bully can in fact punch me in the eye. But the promise breaker is in the same situation as the bully—he cannot violate his promise with impunity. The first line of retribution is that he not only evacuates his promise—and thus becomes a liar in addition to whatever else he may be that is contemptible—but at the same stroke he evacuates his moral personhood. And quite like the bully again, the promise breaker temporarily may scorn such bloodless threats and torments. For the moment it may matter little to him that others will not trust him, and he may not live long enough or intelligently enough ever to regret that. More rational scoundrels, however, will learn from his performance. They will honor promises when the cost of violating them seems to be unacceptably high. It behooves the parties of the second part to keep the price of promise breaking as high as possible.

iii. Thus one of the sanctions rendering claims upon promise enforceable is that kind of rationality called *prudence*. Its relationship to the ethical as such is a remarkably complicated matter. Let us endeavor to sail only so close to its complications as may give us a fair glimpse of the terrain beyond the shoals.

So let us say that prudence is a kind of cost accounting. The prudent man tries to foresee and weigh consequences. He has at least one eye open for contingencies. He wants to know how to get from here to there as safely and as economically as possible, because (a) he already knows the value of his objective and (b) he knows what he can afford to expend for it.

It is not otherwise for nations. Prudentially the rulers of the nation must ask—and it is not just one rational option among others—what will happen if they fail to keep their promises to other nations. How long will heaven smile on the treaty breaker? History gives back the answer: not forever, and perhaps not for long. Whatever else this means, it means that the parties of the second part, and perhaps all other interested parties, have a rational stake in making the way of the transgressor as thorny as possible.

So we remember that promises are not only assurances of good things so long as the contract runs; they are also threats of evil things if the contract is broken. Thus prudence in the one case and fear in the other are double sanctions overarching the promise.

iv. Promises are not necessarily moral. One may promise to deliver three ounces of heroin to a friend. In return he may promise to deliver his sister for prostitution. Here the sanctions are a gross quid pro quo, and we are reminded that a mutual-benefit society is not necessarily a high achievement of human community.

Moreover, I may be lured or frightened into making a promise quite beyond my means for keeping it, though the end in view might be morally unexceptionable. Suppose I promise to give three pints of my blood to save a hemophiliac, even though my physical condition will not tolerate the drainage. But the victim of the disease is someone dear to me, and I am frightened by the magnitude of the threat to his life. Should I feel obligated to keep my promise even though to do so may kill me? Or is it not likely that in this situation I have confused the power of a passion with the sanctity of a promise—would I feel as committed if it were a matter of having promised more than I could afford to help feed starving Biafrans?

We ought not to doubt that there are many ways by which promises can be deficiently rational and fall short of the ethical. But it would be wrong-headed to infer that the promise as such is incompatible with the ethical as such. Surely there is moral weight to keeping one's word, other things being equal; a moral weight and not just a prudential one. Trust is the foundation of much else in the moral life. Indeed, trustworthiness can be achieved quite independently of promise giving. I may say, "I will do the best I can to see justice done," but that is not a promise; I am simply telling you what my intentions are and indicating that I resolve to stand by them. A person who so comports himself is trustworthy. Here it is the performance along the lines of the posted intentions that creates certain expectations. You may well be disappointed if I let you down, but you do not have an enforceable claim against me. "The best I can" may fall far short both of the desirable and of what hitherto I have been able to do, but you do not have a moral right to sue me for the remainder.

So there are different ways in which rational expectations can be created, and a rational redress for nonperformance is not a real possibility in all of them. The overall demand of rationality is simple perspicuity, so that one such situation can be distinguished from another.

10. Do the rulers of a nation have a right to use the power of the state to pursue ideal aims in dealing with other states? The question is designed to return us to the concept of power.

Take the ideal of justice. Suppose that the leaders of a powerful nation believe that a small and defenseless nation is being treated very badly by one of her neighbors. So they resolve to put a stop to that wickedness not because their own country is threatened directly by it but "because it just isn't right and we do not need to tolerate it." Is this decision legitimate; that is, is this exercise of power within the moral prerogatives of the rulers? Or should we say that they are morally charged to serve only the interests of their own nation?

Sensible answers to such questions require clarity in the concepts of *interest* and, again, of the power of the state.

i. A provisional distinction can be drawn between the interests of the state and the interests of the people. The raison de'être of the state is to guarantee security, peace, and justice to the people. A state can fulfill these obligations only if it is coherent and strong. Therefore the rulers have no right to confuse the principles of order or in any other way to reduce the strength of the state. To this extent, at least, the proposition "The state must always act from self-interest" is true.

ii. The interests of the people are much broader than the interests of the state. So far as the people are rational, they want the minimal values guaranteed by the political order. So far as they are sensitive to the richness of the human heritage and of their own traditions, they want far more than that. And they naturally desire the freedom to pursue their infinitely variegated interests and aims.

So it may come to pass that the people themselves set great store by such things as peace and freedom for others and not just for themselves; and they covet justice for all; and, more generally still, they may want to see benevolence rise to any kind of suffering they believe they have the resources to alleviate.

These ethical attainments may seem likely only for the saints above. It is quite as unrealistic not to recognize them when they occur on earth, however infrequently. Be that as it may, where these interests arise in the people, the rulers politic are thereby confronted with severely taxing decisions. They must determine whether benevolence and kindred virtues come in at a price unacceptably high—that is, in relation to the indispensable political values they are pledged to serve. The people may long for the higher righteousness and pursue it with an unearthly passion. If the rulers of the state do not know that keeping the lower righteousness in reasonable working order is an endless (and often thankless) job, they are not fit to hold office.

11. We have now returned to the beginning to ask how the power of the state ought to be conceived.

i. The power of the state can be likened to potential energy stored in a battery. That energy can be counted on to do a certain amount of work when a circuit wired to it is closed. The flow of energy is ended by opening that circuit.

ii. The virtues of this metaphor are modest but real. The state is best conceived of as an instrument rather than as a metaphysical substance. It matters little here whether we call the state an instrument and creation of the General Will or, more loosely, the way a people has adopted to direct the flow of its energy in the interests of a morally legitimate social order.

iii. The analogy also accents the curious and perhaps unique overlaps of actuality and possibility in the power of the state. At any given moment the leaders of the state can actually do a certain range of things with a realistic sense that in doing them they act for the people. It is also the case that at any given moment doing any one of those things may have become a hollow gesture because the people no longer intend that thing, or they intend it in a radically different way. Moreover, the leaders cannot help but make commitments that they cannot make good on, not because the power in general has failed but because the people in general no longer have confidence in them. Thus part of the power of the state must be understood as the readiness of the people, the governed, to accept the policies of their leaders and the rationales offered by these leaders or by their advocates.

iv. But finally the analogy is radically deficient partly because it inspires or warrants a host of *as though* notions. Despite all that is now in the air about cybernetic models of the human mind, if not of human life entire, we must yet say that the moral agent is the key paradigm for the understanding of the political world. That is to say, "What ought I to do?" takes rational precedence over "How can I get what I want?" True, many policy decisions simply assume an answer to the first question and thus appear to raise to highest eminence the latter one. Such assumptions now seem implausible. So we begin to realize that Pragmatism as a political-ethical philosophy can be trusted only in a period of great social stability. It is a very slender reed in a period of great unrest and upheaval.

Thus such figures of speech as "balance of power," "power vacuums," and the like are only suggestive metaphors. The powers of human life—the very phrase suggests both actualities and potentialities—are not best grasped in images and concepts borrowed from physics, mechanics, hydrostatics, etc. There is nothing in the least mechanical about a balance of power in human affairs. It will not take care of itself; it does not provide neat equations in or for the distribution of energy. To maintain a balance of power, whether among nations or in a microsociety, takes exquisitely acute perceptions, great resourcefulness of imagination, sound judgment, and, last but hardly least, rare courage. None of these is a property of any machine known to man; even in man they are rare enough. An ancient writer asks, "Where is wisdom, that I might find it?" A politician who both lacks it and scorns it deserves to be called a hack. No wonder that such a one is prone to think of himself as a cog in a machine.

III

What is meant by the moralization of power? Our final question calls for certain elementary distinctions.

1. Power (like almost everything else) can be moralized by interpreting its uses as congruent with conventional morals or, obversely, as noncongruent with conventional morals. Thus "Smith is a good politician" may mean simply that he is a good husband, good father, good churchman; and he pays his bills. So he has a good reputation, and it

would be hard to underestimate the importance of that in conventional morality. But it is also part of conventional wisdom to believe that Smith will become a shady character if he stays in politics long enough, or a native shadiness will eventually out unless he becomes very powerful and can afford the screening to conceal it or the facade to glamorize it. Thus the "immoralities" of John F. Kennedy have been moralized in the latter mode for popular consumption if not for general emulation.

2. Power can also be moralized by offering specious ethical arguments for its uses to gull the people steeped in conventional morality. This is a common view of Machiavelli's doctrines. The Prince is beyond "good and evil," but he may find it expedient in one situation or another to garb his actions and embellish his policies with moral sentiments.

This is not the place to have it out with this general view of the prince of the kingdom of realpolitik, but I cannot resist making two observations: (a) Machiavelli may have a dialectical view of the prescribed amoralism of the Prince; the ruler's transcendence of good and evil may spring from a realistic rather than a cynical perception of the shallowness of conventional morality. (b) Machiavelli himself subscribed to certain ideal aims, notably to the unification of all Italy, and was a diplomat of exemplary sagacity and fidelity for many years. Florence, his native city, did not reward him very handsomely for this.

3. Power can be moralized by offering bona fide ethical arguments for its uses. Here there is a double assumption: (a) There are no grounds (either theoretical or experiential) for supposing that all ethical arguments are specious; (b) there are some people who will use their rational capacities to appraise ethical arguments.

4. Moralizations of this order are of two kinds, not in respect to their logical structure but in respect to their use. (a) Ethical arguments may be offered as justifications for a way in which power has been used. "I did the right as God gave me to see the right" is (or was) a conventional form of such a justification. Its intention is hardly to put the real responsibility on God. (For that matter, and for all we know, God may feel, "I did what I could to make him see the right.") Of course it is possible that this good man and true did not perceive the right very clearly, and the consequences may have been catastrophic. It does not follow that his line of ethical justification is a flat failure or is any kind of ethical failure. He may have been a very inept fellow, but that does not make him a moral reprobate.

A stronger ethical case can be made against this inept fellow, who ought not to have been given the reins of office in the first place. It is of course unfortunate that he did not see the right very clearly; but that he did not try to correct his vision is far worse; and, worse still, he could not make out any rational connections linking his vision, defective though it was, with practical policy. So of him we are obliged to ask: Was he really trying to do his duty, narrowly as he conceived that, or was he trying to protect his hide from moral abuse when he said, "I did the right as God gave me to see the right"? It can be assumed that "doing one's duty" entails designing and actualizing a viable policy for the right thing.

(b) Ethical arguments may be advanced as incentives for using power one way rather than another. Justifications are *retroflective*. Incentives are *prospicient*. The distinction is theoretical; concrete cases may be obdurate. For example, some ethical justifications are tilted in the direction of saying, "Given the circumstances, I contend that any man of goodwill and perspicuous judgment would do what I did (or tried to do)." This may be the covert appeal: "Whoever in the future finds himself in such circumstances will be justified in doing what I did."

On the other hand one might say, in advancing an ethical argument, "Here is the way to maximize the good under any circumstances. This way lies peace and prosperity for the people and a lasting memorial for the ruler." For doing one's duty may be the highest ethical principle, but there is nothing in itself unseemly in seeking the approbation of the people or in enjoying, either in prospect or in the present, the happy lot into which sagacious governance and benign chance have led them. Indeed, we should have every right to think ill of any concept and theory of power that ignored or disguised the actual drives and incentives without which the ethical life would be a tissue of illusion. No matter how alluring, illusions are benign only so long as they are not or cannot be known to be illusions.

EPILOGUE

I wonder whether we have ever known a time when moralistic attitudes in high places of government made any neater conjunction with widespread cynicism about the amorality of political power. Perhaps we need a new Machiavelli, to help us distinguish superficial and self-serving moralistic postures from authentic ethical commitments, and to show with what fatal ease expediency is disguised as prudence and prudence as the chief end of *homo politicus*.

But there are too many bush-league Machiavellis surrounding the princes of power. Worse still, where monarchs once maintained jesters to inject levity with the fangs of ridicule and irony, our own recent head of state had a court preacher to preserve intact a moralistic, anachronistic pietism against all comers.

Well, perhaps hope has a future as a this-worldly political virtue.

9
Christianity and Politics

The realm of politics has again become a Christian theological concern. Since the theological-political work of Reinhold Niebuhr has not been far offstage any time in the last thirty-five years, the use of "again" may seem a bit odd. But it is the case that in recent times systematic theologians have been more interested in Niebuhr on Sin as Pride, for instance, than in his political theology. In respect to the latter, it might pardonably be said that when the theologians forsook him the social scientists and philosophers took him up; a special panel on his political thought was announced for the 1974 meeting of the American Political Science Association.

So "again" means, largely, that continental theologians in these later years have been forging one kind or other of political theology, either as an extension of a theology of hope that has not yet revolutionized the theological world—perhaps its substance, also, is reserved for some other world—or as part of an ongoing program of showing that Thomism deserves something better than its present desuetude.

In what follows, the continental developments are not the focus of attention; nor is Niebuhr's thought as such. Nonetheless I start with one of his fundamental theological-ethical principles: the tension, in the Christian context, linking justice and love. In *The Interpretation of Christian Ethics* he treats love as a counsel of perfection; but he argues that this must not be grasped nondialectically, as Christian—and other—perfectionists do. In the conditions of historical existence, justice admits of proximate and contingent realization at best; but it has an inescapable claim upon human society. It is a claim that can be honored in some degree or other by social policy and political maneuver. Love, on the other hand, is driven off the stage of public policy into the motivational life of the faithful Christian, the same being a dense thicket of ambiguities. So justice stands forth as the foremost ethical business of the political order, and love as the most excellent reason, the loftiest of inclinations, for seeing that as much justice is done as the historical situation allows.

In what follows in this chapter, I have not pursued Niebuhr's views either to vindicate or rout them. I should want, however, to say that what is everlastingly to be honored in his unrelenting effort to trace a strong, indeed an indestructible, connection of the lower righteousness and the higher righteousness of the Gospel of Jesus Christ: the one the obligation, or range of obligations, of the citizen, the other the high calling of the Christian.

Faithfully and rightly to trace this connection is a formidable undertaking in the intellectual-spiritual climate of contemporary culture; Niebuhr certainly knew this. What, for instance, is more natural than to assume that the contents of the lower and the higher righteousness are alike culture-bounded and culture-determined? For the contemporary American the demand of justice is that he or she must do something, or at least not interfere with things being done, to ameliorate conditions caused by racial discrimination, for example. "Be as just as possible" obviously requires a determination of the possibilities. These are not constant from one age of a society to the next, let alone constant from society to society. And what about the love "commandment" (as though love could be commanded!)? Does not its real meaning rest upon an empirical determination of what persons are in need of love? It is a fine thing to speak of the pure gratuity of love, but suppose it is given as indiscriminately as it is freely? It is also a fine thing to think of everybody as needing love, but surely some people need it more than others.

Well, it is obvious that to be properly empirical about the "need for love" we should have to be explicit and clear about "love." The secular world seems to be in better shape, relative to that, than the church. The former operates generally from a conviction, perhaps we ought to say an axiom, that love is an ego-nurturing activity, or a disposition to that end, either in a human subject or a human object or, just possibly, both. In the church, love seems generally to be viewed and pursued as a genial sentiment given to floating harmlessly above the hurly-burly of the actual world, a winsome thing but vapid, if not inane.

Other ways in which the sociocultural determination of the content both of the higher and lower righteousness is often taken for granted could easily be adduced; it may be doubted that others would be more depressing. But there is the further matter of the way in which the connection of the one ethic with the other is to be viewed. One way of specifying that is to say that the maximum achievement commanded by the higher necessarily waits upon the achievement of the lower. Suppose, for example, that a given society has achieved a comparatively high level of justice (or perhaps we ought to say a comparatively broad or comprehensive justice) through—among other things—a systematic and intelligent nonreligious cultivation of fellow feeling. What is the Christian moralist to make of that situation?

He might say (1) that fellow feeling is what the Gospel means by love. Or he might suggest (2) that this (largely) just society is really a product of God's grace and not of (merely) human insight, ingenuity, and courage; and not at all a matter of luck, therefore. So let us be humbly grateful rather than faithlessly proud. But it might also occur to the Christian that (3) this happy and blessed state of affairs will not last forever; what has? When it is seriously threatened by a mighty external foe, say, or when it begins to disintegrate for other reasons, it will be seen then how steady and generous fellow feeling is. But depressed by such a surly sentiment, the Christian might declare that (4) Christian love must go much deeper into the soul than such natural sentiments and dispositions as fellow feeling and the whole order of (merely) human affections. The love commanded by Christ is a way of grasping and expressing essential humanity. Therefore the proper object of this love is the human community rather than some empirical state of affairs, no matter how sublime for its beneficiaries, falling short of that.

It does not behoove us to come to rest on any of these options now. Let us note, rather, that each of them—though each of them differently—makes both an affirmation and a negation: the higher righteousness is something like what Christian people are doing or what a Christian society has achieved; it is also unlike any of those or that, too. Thus any concrete connection, concrete and faithful, between the two orders of righteousness seems to be as culture-bounded and culture-determined as the "fillings" of the two ethical orders.

The most compelling objection to this conclusion is that it invests heavily in a theory, or a range of theories, about the relationship of culture and social forces to the individual. There is a more modest and realistic alternative. That is simply to say that the Christian concept of a higher righteousness requires perceptiveness and perspicuity on the part of the Christian moral agent. The faithful Christian tries "to serve the present age" as its needs and possibilities demand. So the servant of Christ tries to the utmost to discern the needs and possibilities of the living souls with whom he shares a world. For while it is true that souls always need saving, it is also true that the great destroyers of spirit and community are legion and each has myriad disguises.

So I have begun by assuming that the traditional distinction between natural and supernatural virtues must be provisionally bracketed. The same provisional fate must be visited upon the traditional view that one order is calculated to fit the soul for life on earth and the other for life in heaven. This is not done from any fashionable skepticism about heaven or because I suppose that any supernaturalism is sure to be rejected by the gullet of contemporary sophisticates. The Christian cause would indeed be a forlorn one if the alimentary canal of contemporary culture were the decisive norm of theological validity or of any other kind of health.

No; the bracketing proposed above is simply a dictate of the desire to find—or any rate devoutly to pursue—an ethical unity in the mind and heart of the Christian and the church as together they embrace the world as the object of God's righteous love.

II

How are faith, hope, and love, the traditional supernatural virtues in the Christian context, to be related to politics in the American scene? It is neither necessary nor profitable to dwell at any length on the hazards lying in wait for any serious attempt to answer this question. The situation of the church and the condition of the secular world do not allow us responsibly to avoid it. Moreover, not even the most devout meditation on the venerable theme of Law and Gospel would be likely to meet this need, partly because there are still too many of us who believe that to be for the Gospel entails being against the Law; as though being "delivered from bondage to the Law" is the same as being entirely freed from the claims of the Law. The antinomian option had to be contested in New Testament times. It has lived on and on. It has occasionally achieved a lofty intellectual dignity, such as when it appeals to an ethical principle nobler and more creative than Obligation: Love, for example.

Both in the ancient world and in our own the religious rejection of Law (=rule-bound obligation) makes common cause with a spiritualistic dissolution of the actual world in which moral decisions have to be made and justified. In our time this spiritualistic outlook is likely to appear as the rejection of the impersonal world of massive social structure, the inhuman system of which creative spirit cannot be the creator. This gnosticism purged of archaic mythology elevates the small worlds of free and intense personal relationships as the model of divine intent and the ultimate pattern of human fulfillment.

The gravest element in the Christian flight from the Law is the havoc it wreaks in the understanding of politics and in political participation. It may reasonably be doubted that Christian antinomianism in the American context is likely to inspire acute immorality, though it is certainly available as an excuse for random behavior and self-indulgence. We cannot be so charitable in evaluating its impact on Christian attitudes toward politics. Politics cannot be spiritualized. Its structural features cannot be dissolved into "situation"; nor can they be personalized without remainder. If the Christian feels really called to enter the political realm, he/she ought to be prepared to become partly anonymous thereafter. One ought to be prepared to tend to sores in the body politic by routines that offer little scope for uniquely Christian charismata, routines that cannot be subsumed under the I-Thou category. Spiritualistic antinomianism encourages people to overlook these actualities. Therefore it ought to be opposed more stoutly for this than for its persistent presumption that genuinely illumined souls do not feel any guilt for such indulgences as fornication, masturbation, etc., since the illuminati have been delivered from bondage to the immature prejudices of the unleavened mass.

Thus our first thesis is that becoming "a new man" in Jesus Christ does not dissolve the full-bodied involvement of the Christian in the lower righteousness. By virtue of the transcendent ethical qualities of faith, hope, and love, the dedicated Christian accepts an augmented responsibility in and for the lower righteousness. Thus by virtue of faith, hope, and love the Christian ought to be or aspire to become a transcendently political creature.

"Transcendent" and "transcendently" are not intended to shift discourse to the metaphysical plane. Transcendent ethical features are those which signify the ultimate dimensions of the moral life in the conditions of earthly existence. The transcendently political is that which shows most clearly and definitively what the political order is all about. The central thesis proposed above requires now an examination of the transcendent ethical principles of faith, hope, and love.

III

Faith. The first ethical function of faith (throughout the Christian context is assumed) is to call attention to the fiduciary community in which God and man are united by God's grace. (Fiduciary has a legal ring to it. That is not accidental.) Thus faith is not first of all a readiness to credit historical statements about Jesus Christ or theological statements about God as true. From this it does not follow that faith-as-belief is either banned from authentic Christian existence or rendered menial if not trivial. If one does not believe that God has created the fiduciary community and is everlastingly present in it, one can hardly relate faithfully to it. On the other hand, believing that there is such a community is not yet a concrete relationship to it. That concrete relationship requires decision. Thereafter it demands resolution (courage). This does not mean that faith primarily is a human ability to express and receive trust. That too is involved, but faith is first the situation in which a human being has been put by God's fiducial disposition. Paul says that faith is first God's laying hold of us and thereafter it is our laying hold of him. So the covenant community originates absolutely with God; God in his perfect freedom calls the fiduciary community into being. In and through that, God unalterably keeps faith with man. Man's faithlessness, his repeated violation of the conditions of that community, does not dissolve or diminish that community. This graceless behavior puts a real strain on it (cf. Hosea 13:4-14), but the community belongs to God and he will not relinquish it to any other power or let it go into darkness and silence. Though God is rightly wrathful against his faithless children, he will not always chide.

Thus in the fiduciary community God, the party of the first part, and man, the party of the second part, are bound everlastingly together by pledge and promise. Man could not have created that community. He is called into it. He is thus given the incredible and terrible decision to make: to accept or reject the divine summons. He is ordained for life in the fiduciary community. Only there is man's life rightly ordered; there, and there only, can he come into his true and proper inheritance. But he can do that only by hearing and responding to the Call.

The Law presupposes the covenant community. It is the basic moral structure of that community. The Law is also the basic liturgical structure of that community.

Neither the existence nor the meaning of consentual society, of which the fiduciary community is the highest realization, is effectively denied or even seriously obscured by anything issuing from the arena of metaphysics. There Christian theologians have long contended with the issues of Freedom and Determinism, sometimes as the martyrs and sometimes as the lions. For example, "prevenient grace" has been made to do service as a sort of metaphysical explanation of the life of the faithful Christian. It is a profound mistake to make God's grace into an efficient cause accounting for the existence of the fiduciary community. When "irresistible" is added to grace, the door is opened to emanations from the metaphysical depths which threaten to seize faith in an iron and essentially pagan determinism. That grace should ever have been subjected to such metaphysical brutalities is one of the seven wonders of religious and intellectual history. Surely we have God to thank that the possibilities and demands of the fiduciary community are not thereby diminished or its intelligibility ruined forever by these metaphysical misfortunes. For the grace of which the New Testament speaks is that superabundance of creative love whose motions create possibilities out of nothing and lure creaturely spirits into their realization. Thus grace is the transcendent realm of freedom into which human life is summoned.

If then we must think of grace as a cause, we must find a concept or image of cause free of the least hint of mechanical determinism. Augustine surely knew this as a triumphant Paulinizer of Christian existence: By faith are we saved and not by works of our natural love and design. But he did not keep his hand out of the metaphysical pool. He fished out of it the first asymmetrical and unilateral voluntarism in Western history: The absolute will of God accounts for all that is—except for the evil will of man. This he left without metaphysical explanation because the only one consistent with unilateral theological voluntarism makes God the ultimate source of evil, a view he would not accept on any account. As he sees it, all that God has done is natively good; this is not true of all God consents to.

So faith ought to be protected against even the best-intentioned drafts upon metaphysical explanation, and particularly when these explanations incorporate causal principles whose consistent application would either ruin the religious integrity of faith or leave it standing as a religious offense to an otherwise inclusive explanatory schematism; that is, as a miracle.

Two interrelated things are at stake here: (1) the primordial freedom in which God creates the fiduciary community and (2) the call to participation which God extends to human beings. Faith to faith. "By faith Abraham obeyed when he was called to go out to a place which he was to receive as an inheritance; and he went out, not knowing where he was to go [Heb. 11:8]." "By faith" is not found in the Genesis narrative (12:1). Nevertheless, it is a reasonable interpretation. It also provides a warrant for taking a modest step or two beyond it. Which is to say that Abraham does not behave like a man in the grip of an obsession or like one driven by an irresistible external force. He is "obedient to a heavenly vision." He is a "knight of faith" because wholeheartedly he takes up a summons into the fiduciary community. Thus he, rather than Adam, is the human father of the covenanted people. He, rather than Adam or Noah or Seth, is retrievable and manageable as a historical hero of faith, whether or not contemporary historiography is converted or invoked for such a purpose.

Hope. Hope is the divine reformation of human wishes and expectations for the great and final future wrought only in the fiduciary community, which is both the context of hope and its central focusing object. Thus hope too is a gift of grace, a work of the Holy Spirit. Properly to credit this and live in and by it does not require endorsement of any metaphysical theory about it. More important still, we need not suppose that hope, an infinitely precious gift of God, is a superstructure erected upon and towering over plain and simple natural virtues. God the Spirit pervades the entire structure of human existence, sacred and secular, private and corporate. He is the author of every great expectation. Of course even the most profoundly sincere natural wishes may quarrel with the hope of Christ's kingdom; this applies quite as well for many hopes in and for the church as it does to pagan dreams of greatness and immortality. But in the church the gospel of the kingdom is always at hand for the judgment and reformation of every hope. So far as the church is the faithful servant of the fiduciary community, true hope is part of the common substance of the life in Christ.

Hope is therefore part of "the calling with which we are called." Neither the object nor the context of hope is man's invention. Yet the power by which we lay hold of that object and seek to relate it to the life of the whole world is transcendently human. Nothing is more singularly human than the power by which the potentiality of hope is actualized; nothing expresses any more clearly what one is by one's resolve. No matter how alluring the End, the object of hope, it exists in me in its proper glory only when I weave it into the fabric of my existence and my world.

Let it be said again here that what is at stake in such acknowledgments of human agency is not the fortune or fate of a metaphysical theory. In the fiduciary community, nothing is more important than the proper identification of the personal agents who make it up. In fact, the denser the network of relationships in that community, the greater the significance of personal identity. That community is enriched only by the intensification of individuality. Thus is it not a matter of the first importance to be able properly to affix credit, blame, or honor for things that happen in that community? Towering over these imputations and attributions is the unique joy produced by being able to acknowledge the singularity of contribution each member makes to the common life; for each such freewill offering, and all taken together, are so many ways in which God is glorified.

Love. Love is the power by which the faithful person binds himself or herself to the members of the fiduciary community. Love is the disposition to offer oneself for the "upbuilding of all." Love as a desire aroused in a subject, a person, by certain qualities of an object is love most susceptible to causal explanation, theological and other. Love as the disposition to pledge oneself to seek the good of others is love least susceptible to causal explanation—this love is not aroused, provoked, or stimulated; it is solicited, invited, invoked: summoned. Obediential love can be commanded because the command can be backed with powerful sanctions, of which the most common is, "If you don't obey me I will withdraw my love from you."

We may object to this elementary analysis by saying that obedience can be thus enforced but not love. Would that it were so! The sad and too often tragic truth is that the need for love is so great that one may accept it, perhaps even crave it, on the harshest terms imaginable, even at the cost of the last vestige of freedom. But the highest reaches of loyalty cannot be commanded. One reason for this is that no appropriate sanction is available to be invoked to back a threat against their failure. Another reason is that loyalty transcendent is meaningless except as an expression of freedom. To be sure, I can say, "If you are not loyal to me I will not be loyal to you," but if this is the best I can do I have fallen far short of the highest reaches of loyalty. It is also the case that I may be already savoring the benefits for myself to be achieved by dissolving a fiduciary relationship; so the threat hardly does more, and certainly nothing more dignified, than to call attention to motives already in place to excuse a breach of faith.

The highest reaches of love are expressions of freedom. They cannot be extracted or sustained by threats of any kind. God's love for man expresses the perfection of his freedom as well as the depth of his solicitude for the world. In the perfection of this love, God commits himself to man in a promise. So also a person binds himself to others in an analogous freedom for which *decision* is far more telling than *choice*. The law of love requires me to make decisions in behalf of people some of whom, perhaps many of whom, I would not choose as bosom companions; nor do I have reason to suppose that they have elevated or would elevate me to the top of their heart's desires, either. But of course the fiduciary community is infinitely more inclusive than the circles and bonds of friendship. So too the law of love is infinitely more demanding and more costly than "Be friendly to all and sundry." The face of Jesus Christ, in which Paul professed to have found the likeness of God, is turned toward all mankind in infinite mercy united with infinite suffering. It is not the face of a "friend of man," for that is a mask many have seen fit to wear to disguise an infinite variety of unloveliness.

Thus faith, hope, and love are consental. They are also gifts of the Holy Spirit. They are given from freedom to freedom for the building up of the whole community. That society is a consental order vastly more inclusive than the church.

IV

The Christian believes that the demands and possibilities of the higher righteousness have been made known in Jesus Christ. This righteousness is judged to be higher because it factors more elevated values into the purview of the faithful (or perhaps it also makes these values available to ethically sensitive persons generally). But this is not the only reason for calling the demands and possibilities of the gospel of the kingdom of Christ the higher righteousness. The prime reason for that is that "the righteousness of the kingdom of God" places the heaviest weight and highest value on the exercise of freedom.

This does not mean that the structures of the lower righteousness are simply the pedestal ordained for the grace-full superstructures of transcendent spirit. Idealistic loftiness of mind and apocalyptic debasement of the lower righteousness are both enemies of Christian authenticity.

Thus an initial distinction between the two orders of righteousness emerges. The one is lower because the synthesis of freedom and coercion it demands is relatively simple. The other is higher not because it eliminates in principle every element of coercion but because it demands a far more complex synthesis of freedom and obedience; not intellectually or conceptually complex but existentially and ethically complex.

The political order is the element of the lower righteousness most decisively involved with the common good, the general welfare. Economic systems, everyday morals, the family as a social unit—these too are structures of the lower righteousness. None of them carries the traffic which political structures must bear. This roots in the very nature of the lower righteousness. Here is a sketch of that.

A society levies minimum requirements upon its members. These requirements are the conditions indispensable for the preservation of that society and its culture. Ordinarily these demands of the lower righteousness make thin or weak demands on personal creativity. Some of these requirements are explicitly legislated; accordingly, these are backed with stated sanctions, i.e., penalties for noncompliance. But a willing and cheerful heart in their performance cannot be required. It may be politic to smile at the tax collector; there is no law against scowling at him. Some of the requirements and coercions of the lower righteousness are atmospheric rather than statutory or formulated in rules. We think here of social expectations backed with nonjuridical sanctions of public approbation or disapprobation and perhaps by subjective feelings of acceptance or rejection.

Whether or not a society is a political democracy and represents itself as consentual from top to bottom, its first demands are unavoidably coercive; failure to comply with these primitive demands warrants punishment. On the other hand, no civilization rests its lower righteousness on physical coercions alone. Indeed, it is a commonplace criterion of social advancement that psychological coercions come largely to supplant the use of force. In something like this vein, the arts of persuasion are deemed more worthy of ascription to Deity than the exercise of raw power.

It is also a commonplace that psychological coercion can be as degrading as the brutal instruments of terror. It is far more insidious than the latter. This is particularly true of psychological coercions that have become atmospheric, circumambient, and all-pervasive.

The atmospheric requirements of the lower righteousness seem to be expanding in contemporary life. Middle-class morals (aims, precepts, rewards and punishments) are a sterling case in point. Once upon a time to be an egregious sinner was to invite juridical prosecution as well as ostracism from the company of the righteous and godly. Then there comes a time when it is no longer necessary or even plausible to invoke statutory penalties against a sin as egregious as adultery; it was enough, and more than enough, to brand the culprit a fallen woman, "a lost lady."

On the other hand, it is folly to diabolize the psychological sanctions of the lower righteousness. Human life is meaningless, it is but an episode in the mammalian world, unless it is pursued and realized within humanly determined boundaries. Moreover, ideally the psychological coercions of a social order constitute an element in the internal structure of the moral agent. One ought not to do the things that incur guilt even though an iron fist is not posed above one's head. More especially still, one ought not to do things that diminish or debase the lives of others or weaken the fabric of one's society—which is also to say that the primitive boundaries of the lower righteousness are not absolute; they are not divine edicts. They are not there to curtail aspirations for a richness and power of life far transcending a standard existence. They are there to control impulses and ambitions that in their exercise diminish the lives of others and make the lower righteousness appear to be the blessing of the weak and the curse of the strong.

In American society, powerful atmospheric pressures have long been accumulating around a great many things beside conventional morals. Much of the radical dissent of the sixties was directed against psychological coercions to adapt much if not all of one's individuality to the requirements and expectations of "middle America." The protest often adopted bizarre and unproductive forms (socially unproductive; they may have had considerable ventilator benefit) because the atmospheric pressures of the conventional order defied discrimination of authentic moral demands from unrelenting insistence to conform to parental expectations. The standard goodies were supposed to be available only to the adaptable. That kind of conformity seemed too high a price to pay for satisfaction so trivial. Thus radical protest was quite willing to become, quite literally, a stench in the nostrils of the righteous; for the first time in the history of religion, prophets assumed that clean hands and a pure heart were necessarily related by inverse ratio. It may be doubted that this prophetic posture opened new spiritual vistas to the world's millions who were and are necessarily dirty, unkept, unkempt, and uncared for.

During the sixties the radical critics commonly assumed that the general political order was hopelessly implicated in the conventional value system. More specifically, the American engagement in Vietnam was viewed as a terrible triumph of middle-class moral obtuseness, provincialism, and decadence. At the same time many defenders of the conventional value system just as devoutly believed that politics as such is a dirty business, an order of things far more vulnerable to moral corruption than the business world or any other sector of modern life. The prize for consistency—however one assesses that—goes to the middle-classer at that point, since he viewed with deep suspicion first and then with bristling hostility the prophetic proclamation of an ethics stripped of all absolutes—except for the fiery prophet's divinely passionate denunciation of a war that was absolutely immoral.

Nonetheless radical dissent had a point. The rhetoric of politics then reeked with moralistic odors: "the national honor," "service above the call of duty," "honoring our commitments," etc. The great mass of people has generally credited these appeals when the fate of the nation seems to hang in the balance. During the engagement in southeast Asia it was not easy to believe that the national interest was so absolute; honor, trustworthiness, a barrier to Communist aggression, yes; but not life or death, power or impotence. But the critics of the Left could hear only cynicism and deadly sentimentality in this rhetoric.

However when the issues before the nation were internal justice, relief of needless suffering, and the like, there were some striking inversions in the ways people appraised the rhetoric of politics. Now many defenders of the conventional value system were threatened by idealistic liberal rhetoric while the prophets of the Left insisted that this rhetoric now had the bite and authority of Reality; it had to be cashed out, if necessary at the expense of international commitments and national security. Spokesmen for radical dissent now took up the idealistic rhetoric with which to chastise the national political leadership; it had stripped the nation of the last shred of rectitude and dignity. But middle grounders and conservatives expressed dismay and alarm as they began to count the cost of putting the domestic house in order; the dollar cost, yes, but also the loss of local and personal decision to megalithic and megalomaniacal politics.

The unique responsibilities of the Christian in this situation seemed terribly ambiguous. The lower righteousness had become virtually identical with the conventional value system. Yet the righteousness of that system was under very heavy fire. It still is. Indeed, a good word in its behalf may succeed only in plugging the ears of the rising generation against any faithful word about the impingement of a higher righteousness upon the lower. But to start at the top—that is, to begin with the higher righteousness in abstraction from the lower—is to encourage an antinomianism and anarchism already puissant in contemporary life. So the Christian prophet may find it very difficult on the one hand to argue cogently and persuasively that civil disobedience is a legitimate instrument of the higher righteousness, and on the other hand to discourage, as cogently and persuasively, the use of drugs of scientific dubiety to discover or expand the Real Self. The ethical legitimation of extraordinary instruments for turning public policy from immorality and folly toward rectitude and wisdom is a desperately important matter. Is it more important than the emergence—or should we say resurrection? —of real persons from conventional fictions and self-deceptions?

V

It is not my intention to write a preface for A Plain Christian's Guide Through the Moral Jungles of the World. I do now intend to call attention to some things a Christian can say for which he or she may have unique motivation. It is possible, also, that a Christian may come up with some unique propositions about the moral life. But first a homely observation or two.

For example, a value system is not wrong merely because it is conventional. To say of a system that it is conventional is, firstly, to say it is a public rather than a private system. Secondly, the fact that a value system is conventional means that one can find one's way through the world with its assistance; that is, thanks to conventional morals one can make choices and in general get on with making and enjoying a life without plunging into the depths of reflective reason every time a moral decision and a moral judgment must be made. Only a thinker in love with a portrait (perhaps a self-portrait) of Man as Rational will object to a conventional system on this count. Thirdly, it is not the conventional value system as such that discourages profound and searching reflection upon moral decision and moral judgment. Objections to the conventional system are themselves objected to by people who of course have made heavy investments of identity, dignity, and status in the conventional system. Prima facie their motives are as respectable as the motives of the critics of the system; or, if you prefer, as dubious; but in either case, no more so. No doubt the prophetic frenzy and poetic power of Nietzsche may lead us to suppose that his case and its arguments *must* be superior to stodgy Bishop Butler's. That *must* has little to do with rationality.

The unique motive available to the Christian for making these plain observations is simply the Christian principle that the critic of the value system is just as vulnerable to the virus of self-righteousness as its stodgiest defender. Happily, however, this is only part of the Christian motive. We ought also to count as part of that the hope that critic and defender alike will come to see that both of them are investing sur-value in the minimum system. Both are overloading the conventional order. One overloads it by making it demonic. The other overloads it by making it the way, the truth, and the life—by making it the one indispensable foundation for righteousness in the sight of God. The one sees only the inhumanity of the system. The other sees only its security, its affluence, and the scope it offers for solo performances of kindness and generosity, at home and afield.

Therefore the Christian ought to remember that the primary function of the conventional ordering of life is not to make men righteous, either by forcing them to conform to it or by conscientiously opposing it. Rather the primary task of the conventional system is to civilize the human creature according to a model and rule of civilization. Model and rule together constitute the code of that civilization.

What then should the Christian as Christian say about that code? First: No code should be held to be given directly by God unless it is the ethical extract of a unique communal relationship to God. The Old Testament is a uniquely significant document for this very reason; it contains several different extracts from one and the same unique communal relationship to God—the Law and the Prophets. The Law becomes a wonderfully complex and humanly rich code within Judaism, a miraculously perdurable religious culture within a staggering succession of hostile civilizations. In Old Testament times the Lord raised up the prophets mightily to assail such corruptions of his code as the blandishments of heathen cultures or the harrowing vicissitudes of history might propose. It is thus one of the more remarkable paradoxes of religion in the modern world that "prophecy" should come to signify postures and programs calculated to discredit or displace any confidence in any code save the regimen of a nuclear revolutionary society. So the contemporary prophet is likely to view the tension between Priest and Prophet in ancient Israel as the glorious promise of a total alienation of the higher righteousness from the lower.

Secondly, however, may it not be the case that for the faithful Christian the most significant criticism of the established order is the one which most clearly expresses an earnest and settled intention to change it? If this is so, then the validity of any New Testament model is seriously compromised if not ruined altogether. Consider Paul as a case in point.

It is not unreasonable to commend Paul for not having rallied the Christian communities around the Roman Empire to an all-out attack upon slavery. Or should we be more circumspect in respect to our own libertarian sentiments and simply say, for instance, that imperial Rome had not incorporated into the code of civilization what we commonly accept and affirm as the freedom of the individual? No doubt that was a radical defect in the system; whether it was a prime factor in Rome's eventual collapse is a different question. Moreover, we cannot legitimately charge off Paul's failure to attack slavery as an institution to a radical eschatological foreshortening of history, since it is generally supposed that he fell back from the apocalyptic expectations of his earliest writings; in any case we do not find in him the sort of demonizing of Roman civilization so visible in the lurid apocalypticism of Revelation. Surely the vital element for Paul is his conviction that the magistrate rules by the consent of Almighty God (Romans 13). Paul does not generalize from this a blanket of sanctity for the entire social system; he does not say that God approves of imperial society! On the other hand it is apparent in Paul's account that God does approve of order, and to that extent civilization operates with a kind of divine license; it is preferable to barbarism. Some of the institutions of civilization may be brutally inhuman, but if Romans is a fair sample Paul thought the effects of social disorganization were more offensive in the sight of God. Moreover, the social system provided for the release of some from slavery: the freedmen. For whatever it may be worth, we may say that if that structural modification had not antedated the Christian movement Paul would have lacked some of the powerful metaphors with which he interprets the saving work of Jesus Christ.

We must also ask what kind of model of a Christian social revolutionary is the Christ of the Gospels, either in precept or example. Some Marxists have had an answer to that, but the Jesus who appears in that is a pure synthetic product of dialectical materialism. Over against all such fugitive representations of Christ, the dominant traditions of the church long ago crystallized around the conviction that as the Prince of the kingdom of God Jesus Christ brings the "permanent revolution" into human history: It is through God's grace that his demands can be met; that is, that every soul and every nation shall offer to him its unique "sacrifice." Being translated, this means that the transformation of any given soul or nation is not designed, in the conditions of historical existence, to render either of them or any of them perfect; the goal of the divine revolution is to clear the tracks for the realization of the common good through the fulfillment of an infinite variety of specific contracts or covenants.

So it is not the case that the most significant criticism of the social order within the range of the faithful Christian is the one which most clearly expresses an earnest and settled intention to change it. Quite to the contrary, the most significant critical work for the Christian to engage in is that of assaying the lets and hindrances obstructing free access to the rights and privileges of this American society. He will find these built into an outrageously large number of institutions. He will find these impacted in his own soul. He will find them as encrustations on the code of this civilization. He will find them as parasites engorging themselves on his courage and willpower.

If the Christian is properly tutored in the traditions of the faith, he will know in advance of these empirical determinations that there are "demons" that yield only to prayer and fasting. Not that these are themselves weapons! Rather, they are the indispensable conditions for keeping hold on faith, hope, and love as one struggles "to do good to all men" so far as one is able so to do.

The code of our civilization incorporates guarantees of personal freedom. This is congruent with the convictions that the political order ought to be truly consentual and consent cannot be coerced. These magisterial convictions are unhappily linked in American sentiments with a dubious piece of metaphysics: Individualism. It is also to be noted that the juridical guarantees of personal freedom do not entail or otherwise permit us reasonably to predict that freedom as an ideal aim will be properly served in or by the code. Personal freedom as granted or acknowledged by law, moreover, by no means guarantees that a genuinely free society will arise if by that we now mean not only a consentual order but an affirmative and creative community: a society in which mature persons affirm and actively pursue the good of all.

The fact that liberty requires statutory guarantees is a powerful reminder of this situation. An agency of society must be ordained to enforce those guarantees. If necessary, that agency must be allowed to amplify its powers for that purpose. If necessary, that agency of the state must be licensed to use force to restrain people who aggrandize themselves at the expense of the rights of others. And so it comes about that people get hurt when liberty is protected against the raiders and poachers; sometimes the victims get hurt and the pirates wax strong and proud. Then there is little use in crying to heaven for relief and vindication. The thing rather to do is to figure out how the pirates can be sunk. There is no use in wondering whether to take up arms against a sea of misfortunes. It makes sense to take aim at the scoundrels who sail thereon. It is odd that a fair number of fine folk think it odd that Christians should think even metaphorically in such martial tones.

It is natural and proper that people in a consentual society should suppose that vigilance in the protection of liberty for all is part and parcel of concern for the public good. Yet in America today there is a good deal of atmospheric pressure circulating in the opposite direction. The theology of the plain man—whoever he is—still inclines to view the public good as an additive result of multiple private goods and special interests. More sophisticated souls deny the "reality" of the concept of the public good. Against these opinions high and low we need to be good-naturedly but firmly dogmatic in demanding that the facts be faced. The grandest of these facts is that the public good is not a composite of private goods; it is the good people can enjoy only by being together, only by being incorporated one way rather than another. A somewhat less grand fact is related to the first one: the state is the skeleton, so to speak, of that incorporation. A political regime is a device for administering the power of the state to maintain the balance of personal rights and public good envisioned and defined by the fundamental law of the land.

A regime may properly employ an ethical rhetoric to discharge its essential function; it is not foreordained that such a regime must tumble straightaway into hypocrisy and deceit. A regime in and of a consentual society ought generally to use the arts of persuasion to preserve peace and pursue justice. Certainly the people ought not to feel insulted if a regime treats them as though they were moral agents. It appears, moreover, that it is one of the high functions of religion in America to move the hearts of the people to obey their leaders if their leaders appear to know what they are doing and have sound reasons for it. Those qualifications have not always been clearly signaled from the pulpits of the land, to be sure, but that does not seem to disqualify or embarrass the empirical generalization that at any rate that is how safe and sane religion generally works.

Christians ought to remember that a really sane religion is not always a safe one publicly to espouse. Regimes and political parties have been known to inflate themselves to the dimensions of semidivinities in wild lusts to control the actions and consciences of the people. Such tyrants do not strain gladly to hear the voice of the prophet of the Lord in the land.

There is no compelling reason for the Christian in America, the land of the free, to think in such stark terms. He or she might more profitably ponder the buildup of psychological coercions, of atmospheric pressures, constraining us—seducing us, indeed—to quarantine the lower righteousness against incursions from the higher, and to let the higher drift off as free-floating high-mindedness and spirituality, a genial fog sum-

moned to obscure the sights, sounds, and stench of a garbage dump.
What should the faithful Christian say and do in that situation?

A persistent idealistic strain in American Christianity may still predis-
pose many of us to answer such a question in terms of the priorities of
an inclusive humanity-wide ethical commonwealth: something like the
Kantian "realm of ends." This idealistic appeal has often passed as the
heart of an authentic Christian criticism of politics and therefore as the
real content of the higher righteousness. This is an important error. The
Gospel does indeed contain a conception of an inclusive humanity, a
community created and sustained by God himself. The fulfillment of
this community—more accurately, the fulfillment of man in this community—is clearly a central element in the exalted hope of the Gospel.
But this community of God and Man revealed in Jesus Christ is not
to be confused with the idealistic projections of the historical life of
mankind or of any humanly exalted fragment thereof. Whence it follows
that the idealistically envisioned ethical commonwealth of mankind is
not the first and highest object of loyalty of the authentic Christian,
though from this it hardly follows that idealistic aspirations in politics
or elsewhere are but "filthy rags" in God's sight.

Thus it is true that the Christian is summoned to acknowledge every
person as a kinsman, as a fully accredited member of the community
of mankind in God; so that whoever is within the perimeters of my
power as a person has a claim upon my love and not just a potential
claim upon my social instinct for justice. But it does not follow that I
must regard that ethical kinsman, that sibling in the divine family, as
endowed with certain inalienable rights in the civil order, rights that
I am *Christianly* obligated to defend from every encroachment from
political tyranny and/or economic coercions. The fact that I am called
of God to love my brothers and sisters in Christ does not necessarily
mean that I am obligated to try to overthrow a social system that
unmercifully oppresses them. Supernaturally great and glorious as the
gifts of the Holy Spirit are, I cannot count on him to make me a David
to bring down Goliath even though the people of God suffer all day long
from the brute.

So naturally and in seemly passion we ask to learn what kind of love
it is that acquiesces in oppression and brutal tyranny. The answer is:
Simply to acquiesce is indeed wrong, and it is worse to offer a pious
baptism to tyranny or to any other form of dehumanizing coercion, be
it statutory or atmospheric. But at the lively risk of outraging legitimate
idealistic and humanitarian sentiments, we must go farther than that

and say that the Gospel does not promise that the always potentially demonic limitations of individual and corporate righteousness will ever be overcome finally in the course of history; or that God will destroy an iniquitous empire to spare the innocent further affliction and degradation.

But neither is there any comfort in the Gospel for the person who bows the neck to tyranny that his own skin and self might be spared. For the good of others and not just for conscience' sweet sake, a time comes when one must do the "works of love" despite the terrors of the regime. And then a time comes when one must consider how an evil regime can be undone most effectively and appropriately. In both times, on all such occasions, there is a dreadfully wide margin of error. Can a hateful (and not just a hated) regime be *loved* to its extinction, in a reasonable time? Or should one faithfully embrace the grave risks of allowing or even encouraging righteous indignation against an evil regime to be replaced by insensate hatred of the Enemy as mortal combat begins?

Put it more concretely. How could a Christian conscience *not* have authorized the violent destruction of the Nazi abomination of desolation once the vastness of its horrid ambitions and the diabolical brutality of its methods had become clear? But there is the counterquestion: How could the authorization for the violent destruction of this wickedness have been made absolute? It was not absolute. It cannot ever be absolute. To ask for that absolute authorization, perchance to dream of it, is grievously to confuse human existence with the divine.

These reflections are reinforced by some considerations from the side of realpolitik. It may be doubted that the nation as a political entity ever acts in relation to other nations or their peoples from idealistic humanitarian motives. As a political entity the nation acts to preserve its own people, and thus the state as such must always seek to reduce or destroy external threats to its own existence. The ways in which the state acts for these interests are inescapably subject to moral judgment, just as a person is called to judgment—both juridical and moral—for the use of excessive force in protecting his own life and interests. But this moral accountability does not convert the state as such into a transcendent ethical reality. The citizen has a right and a duty to hold the regime morally responsible for the ways it has conducted the affairs of state. It does not follow from that that the leaders of the state must pose as exemplars of the Good Man.

These considerations can be expressed in a somewhat different way.

There is no uniform pressure from the realm of Ideality upon persons and societies; there is such pressure but it is not uniform. Thus Justice does not signify an ideal state of human life on earth. Justice is a demand to set a given house in order by the ground rules that make it that kind of house. Peace is not the name of a perfectly harmonious state of human affairs. It is a demand to preserve or restore an equilibrium of forces that alone makes harmony and tranquillity possible in a given time and given way. To add *Christian* as a qualifier to Justice and Peace is not to change the fundamental demand of each; it is not even immediately to substitute one picture of the human community for another, though that is finally involved. Thus the proper force of *Christian* as a modifier in the American context is twofold: (a) it calls attention to the unique covenant this nation has with God (rather than with Ideality) and (b) it says that Justice and Peace are hardly more than the beginning of the Christian's unique obligation and high calling. That is to identify with whoever suffers the human lot. The Christian is called to weep with those who weep and to laugh with those who laugh, but not because weeping and laughing are holy in themselves. What is holy is the bond of community revealed in Jesus Christ and sustained everlastingly by the Holy Spirit. Rightly to honor and rejoice in that bonded relation means that the Christian's concern for others must go far beyond a humane interest in their having the minimal survival existence. Need we pause here to note in this enlightened age that Christian love must not abstract from the minimum? Is it not plain enough as a dictate of common sense that people who are starving cannot be taught how to be free and creative? Enjoining sinners to prepare to meet their Creator is a sober undertaking—it may be an elevated one in the proper context. But so to preach and otherwise to relate to people who have never had a chance to reach a really human level of existence is immoral as well as lunatic.

VI

The higher righteousness stands in the mind and heart of the Christian as a summons to personal engagement with persons as they actually exist and with social forces working to deliver actual persons from the actual and unnatural restrictions upon their creative powers. There is no unique Christian concern for Justice. There is a unique Christian concern for love when love is grasped as the readiness to bear the burdens of others with a view to amplitude of life for all. Should we conclude that the Christian can conscientiously allow his concern for justice and peace to fall below the threshold of conventional morality? Hardly! Where conventional morality encourages or condones acquiescence in massive injustice, it must be rebuked and reformed. That rebuke will not be efficacious if it is simply a mighty blast of denunciation detonated by a fiery, charismatic prophet. Reformation will not be achieved by a committee of idealists. A faithfully prophetic church will make it clear that God demands more than a purging or elevation of the aims, sanctions, and expectations of conventional morality. God demands that personal dispositions and commitments be reoriented. He demands that social structures be modified if their operations and atmospheres are inimical to the true and common good.

How the church ought to go at this proclamation of the Gospel rests largely on accurate perceptions of how people in this society perceive the connections linking conventional morality and social forces that give or take away the "good life." When those forces are perceived to be benign, or perhaps even exquisitely providential, then a "good character" is likely to be widely honored, though perhaps not passionately sought, as a necessary condition for enjoying the "good life." But if social forces are perceived to be inimical or perhaps even maliciously hostile to the "good life," then "good character" may be deemed a hindrance to a properly energetic scramble for security, dignity, power, and affluence in a world perceived to be a moral jungle.

Christian criticism of conventional morality when the latter licenses acquiescence in injustice ought to lead to concerted political action. This is part of the content of "engagement with forces working to free actual persons from the actual and unnatural restrictions upon their creative powers."

"Concerted political action" does not entail the formation of a Christian political party—an affliction America has been largely spared. Christian political action does entail active presence in the arena of political decision—and not merely as a supercharged prophet. Given the realities of the American political system, Christians do not need to settle for simply making a witness before they are flushed down the drain as political irrelevancies. That is to say that the Christian, politically speaking, does not exist merely to be heard. He exists to be felt if not welcomed as a power; he exists to be reckoned with; he exists, if necessary, as a bone crossways in the gullet of his political party. None of this can be done merely by being a highly moral private person. Somebody must also reach for votes. Somebody must find or help to create a like-minded caucus within the party structure. Why should not this somebody be a person energized and not just enlightened by Christian principle? In such roles, to be sure, a Christian may get low marks from people who like their Christians to be purely "spiritual"; that is, being translated, all "heart" and with no head for the social actualities and no guts for conflict. In general the people—and the churches are well supplied with them—who look with marked disfavor upon Christian aggressiveness in politics are the same people who would like to think that there is a clear and important distinction between politics and "power politics"; so of course they believe that a sound Christian would never voluntarily and knowingly become enmeshed in the immoralities, the unconscionable compromise, of power politics.

VII

The eschatological dimensions of the higher righteousness cannot be overlooked or played down in a Christian theology and practice of politics. But what ought we to make of those formidable dimensions of the higher righteousness?

Some possibilities come to mind. (1) In the New Testament the revelation of the higher righteousness is the work of Jesus Christ and as such it is one of the "signs and wonders" of the eternal kingdom of God. Hence the transcendent goodness of life commanded by God through his son cannot be formulated as a code for a novel and holy civilization, nor can it be incorporated into the code of some extant civilization. (2) Christian moralists have sometimes inferred from this that the essential features of Gospel righteousness are so many counsels of perfection and must remain such so long as history runs, as though they were so many divinely created and divinely sanctioned ideal lures forever beckoning persons from stale and deathly habit to high and noble aspiration but forever eluding actualization. This view confuses the realm of Ideality with the severe demands of God Transcendent. God has nowhere revealed impatience with habit as such; that is, with the idea of a conventional morality. So far as we accept Jesus Christ as the absolute revelation of the divine will, we must be so far persuaded that God's demands are never less than the minimum demands of a well-ordered society. But we must also believe that those minimum conditions can be infused with a restlessness that will not allow habit to become stale or deadly. (3) The higher righteousness and its eschatological setting are alike more than a system and a schedule for entrance into heavenly bliss. Together they assure us that we ought never to take life in this world less seriously than God himself has done and will forever do. Thus to respond to the summons of the higher righteousness in Christ, to respond with fear and trembling but above all with a very great joy, all that is a possibility in and for actual existence in this world; for so to do God's will, even though what we accomplish seems finally to us to be so much straw, is the while to participate in God's work in the world and for it; but it is also and above all else to participate in God's life as the in-all and be-all of the blessed community.

VIII

Today the church seems remarkably apathetic, overall, about secular politics. The unleavened mass of the church seems quite content to let prophets true and false do everything they deem requisite to meet the demands of the living God. Quite unlike the Pharisees of New Testament accusation, the unleavened mass of the church seems to be blissfully unaware of the fact that even the prevailing moral code lays weightier matters upon conscience than the rising tide of fornication and drug addiction. But the demands of the higher righteousness run far beyond even the sternest demands of the lower righteousness. Anxiety over loss of social approval or concern for acceptance by one peer group or another—or by several in conflict with one another—may well deaden conscience to the minimal demands of justice. How will the demands of the higher righteousness fare in such a time?

A grand illusion still flourishes throughout the middle ground of the church. There it is still widely believed that the higher righteousness is fulfilled by attaining—or never losing!—purity of motive and by the suppression in oneself of every sign of hostility toward one's neighbors, provided that the neighbors are fundamentally decent people who keep up their property. How can this state of mind conceivably make peace with the "terrible swift sword" of the Gospel? How can it cope with the elemental power of the parable of the last judgment where the accent falls so fiercely upon what the true believer *has done* in behalf of any and all who suffer deprivation? Can we seriously believe that the Lord's demands are met by a series of well-spaced visits to members of the congregation prevented by infirmities of mind or body from attending divine services? Hardly! But neither can we seriously believe that God's demands are met only by cunning and resolute attempts to root out the last vestige of imperial order from the world. Mankind is badly served by imperial orders, but it is not altogether clear that anarchy is preferable to every kind of empire. Some empires have been better than others; Marx admitted that; but that doesn't mean that imperial rule is the best mankind can do. The principle of empire is that "some men lord it over others," they exercise arbitrary authority to make arbitrary allocations of rights and duties, and they acquire honor and glory if they do these things well; but they may acquire power and wealth no matter how badly they do them. Jesus tells his disciples "it is not to be like this among you" (cf. Mark 10:43). This is not a negative definition of either ecclesiastical or civil organization. It tells us how the faithful servants of the kingdom will understand and evaluate honor, power, and glory.

Many chance factors play into the formation of church structures and civil constitution. That does not legitimately strip either of them of providential meaning. This providential meaning does not serve us well when it is misperceived to be a divine legitimation for either ecclesial or civil constitutions. A providential meaning is something that directs attention to a unique covenantal relationship to the living God. It is customary and easy to say that deliverance from a grave national crisis was providential. It is not so easy and it is hardly customary now to say that a severe testing of the fabric of the nation and the attendant trying of the souls of its people is providential; but why should we not say so then if these fiery trials come down to arrest what otherwise might have been an irreversible slide into abysmal depths of injustice?

It is time for the voice of a faithful church to be heard again saying that the divine ordination of any political regime or of the conduct of any regime civil or ecclesiastical does not mean that what it, what any of them, is or is doing meets altogether with God's consent and approval. Regimes both civil and ecclesiastical have often coveted that absolute legitimation. Now we do not hear a great deal of the classical rhetoric of divine legitimation in the political realm. Some of the logic remains; e.g., in appeals to "historical necessity" to legitimatize totalitarian systems. Some of the rhetoric survives to rationalize the perpetuation of imperial ecclesial structures. Some of the longing for an ultimate legitimation lingers in the atmospheric elements surrounding the dogged efforts to preserve the American Way of Life. In the long run the results of these cravings for absolute legitimation are exposed as the conceits of self-aggrandizement, self-righteousness, and an irrational self-protection. The wisdom of the long run is often won at a dreadfully high cost spread out over many generations.

An authentic Christian appeal to the eschatological fullness of the higher righteousness incorporates the long run of history, but not simply that people might become wise by the careful use of retrospective judgment. The latter is the counsel of sober common sense. Faith, hope, and love go beyond that. In the end all shall be judged and found wanting, as God the Father is the Judge of all and Christ the Son is the glory of his righteousness. In the meantime we are not warranted to try to judge as God alone judges. We are authorized and obligated so to order all our affairs that no one within the perimeters of our power is foreclosed from the opportunity to live humanly. So personally and corporately we have many sins both of omission and commission to confess.

God's forgiveness is truly wonderful; he has everlastingly in view the renewal of a human resolution to walk ever in more Godly ways. Practice in this will not bring in the kingdom of God, no matter how inspired and unsparing the practice is. It will help, it will surely help, self and others to learn what that kingdom is all about. For as Christ is our pioneer and our warrant, that kingdom is the prize and joy of all desiring.

ABOUT THE AUTHOR

Julian Norris Hartt, a native of Selby, South Dakota, is a graduate of Dakota Wesleyan University, Garrett Theological Seminary, Northwestern University (M.A.), and Yale University (Ph.D.). From 1932-34 Dr. Hartt served as minister of United Methodist churches in South Dakota. He has taught theology and philosophy at Berea College (1940-43) and Yale University (1943-53), was Noah Porter Professor of Philosophical Theology at Yale University (1953-72), and is now William Kenan, Jr., Professor of Religious Studies, The University of Virginia, Charlottesville. He is the author of numerous articles, essays, and books including *Humanism Versus Theism* (1953), *Toward a Theology of Evangelism* (1955), *Being Known and Being Revealed* (1957), *A Christian Critique of American Culture* (1967), and *Theology and the Church in the University* (1969).